Sherry Knight and **Steven Yoder** are
software and consultants to small businesses looking toward automation. Ms. Knight is a Certified Public Accountant and managing partner with Knight & Co. in Oakland, California; Mr. Yoder holds an engineering degree and an M.B.A.

MICRO-ACCOUNTING

Setting Up Your Books on the Computer

A SPECTRUM BOOK

Steven E. Yoder
Sherry D. Knight

MICRO-ACCOUNTING

Setting Up Your Books on the Computer

PRENTICE-HALL, INC.
Englewood Cliffs, New Jersey 07632

Library of Congress Cataloging and Publication Data

Yoder, Steven E.
Micro-accounting.

"A Spectrum Book"—T.p. verso.
Bibliography: p.
Includes index.
1. Accounting—Data processing. 2. Microcomputers—Programming. I. Knight, Sherry D. II. Title.
HS5679.Y6 1984 657'.028'54 84-17688
ISBN 0-13-580093-5
ISBN 0-13-580085-4 (pbk.)

A Spectrum Book. Printed in the United States of America.

10 9 8 7 6 5 4 3 2 1

A SPECTRUM BOOK

ISBN 0-13-580093-5

ISBN 0-13-580085-4 {PBK.}

Editorial/production supervision by Lori L. Baronian
Cover design by Hal Siegel
Manufacturing Buyer Gary Orso

This book is available at a special discount when ordered in bulk quantities. Contact Prentice-Hall, Inc., General Publishing Division, Special Sales, Englewood Cliffs, N.J. 07632.

Prentice-Hall International, Inc., *London*
Prentice-Hall of Australia Pty. Limited, *Sydney*
Prentice-Hall Canada Inc., *Toronto*
Prentice-Hall of India Private Limited, *New Delhi*
Prentice-Hall of Japan, Inc., *Tokyo*
Prentice-Hall of Southeast Asia Pte. Ltd., *Singapore*
Whitehall Books Limited, *Wellington, New Zealand*
Editora Prentice-Hall do Brasil Ltda., *Rio de Janeiro*

CONTENTS

PREFACE

WHAT THIS BOOK IS ABOUT

This book is an introduction and guidebook for potential users of microcomputer accounting systems. It tells you what micro-accounting can do for you (and what it can't), what it will cost, and how to get past the three hurdles in your way.

Your first hurdle is the decision whether your business will benefit from computerizing. This book offers a cost/benefit analysis, as well as extensive discussion of the potential benefits, limitations, and costs.

Your second hurdle is the selection of the right system from the hundreds available. This book offers a series of criteria lists that will help you analyze your needs and evaluate accounting *software.* There is also extensive discussion of what to look for and to look out for.

Your third hurdle is the set-up and use of the micro-accounting system. This book offers a set of checklists for converting accounting systems and a chapter on standard operating procedures appropriate for computerized systems. There is also an example of the detailed *documentation* appropriate for a new micro-accounting system.

There are lists of accounting software companies, microcomputer magazines, and other books about computerizing. There are copies of forms and checklists to use and a glossary.

WHO THIS BOOK IS FOR

This book is for the businessperson or professional with little or no experience in using computers. If your company is experiencing continuing growth or has some accounting bottlenecks, a microcomputer may provide the increased accounting power you need at a fraction of the cost of previous computer systems.

Computer dealers and salespeople will find the cost/benefit analysis and the criteria lists useful. Computer and business consultants will find the chapters on the *conversion process* and the standard operating procedures helpful. There is also an appendix for professional accountants and bookkeepers who are entering this new and dynamic field.

ACKNOWLEDGMENTS

We would like to thank: all of our micro-accounting clients, for the pleasure of working with them; ComputerLand of Oakland and the many accounting software companies that supported our research for this book; the staff at Prentice-Hall for their support and encouragement, with special thanks to John Hunger for coining the term *micro-accounting;* and our own Nikki Kutulas, for her valuable assistance in the preparation of the manuscript.

Portions of Chapter 3 are taken from a paper published in the *Conference Proceedings of the 1st IBM PC Faire,* published by Computer Faire, Inc., August 1983. The paper was entitled, "Accounting Software for the IBM PC/XT . . . What to Look for," by Sherry D. Knight, CPA.

Portions of Chapter 4 are taken from an article published in the June 1983 issue of *Interface Age* magazine. The article was entitled, "Converting to a Computerized Accounting System," by Sherry D. Knight, CPA.

Portions of the cost/benefit analysis in Section 2.1 are derived from an article published in the February 13, 1984 issue of *Computers & Software News.* The article was entitled, "Analyzing the costs/benefits of Computer Purchases," by Michael Wolff.

INTRODUCTION

I.a WHAT THIS BOOK IS ABOUT

This book is about computerizing the accounting system of a small business. If you are using a manual accounting system (pencil-and-paper journals) or are sending your records to an outside accounting service, then this book is for you. It will show you the great advantages a computerized system has to offer; it will also point out the pitfalls and how to avoid them.

It is written for the beginning computer user, that is, for any accounting department that is considering the purchase of its first computer. We are not going to teach you about microcomputer innards, nor about programming; you no longer have to become a computer design expert to select and use a small computer system. Nor is it necessary to hire a specialized support staff. If you have someone in-house currently doing your bookkeeping, that same person can be trained to do it on the *PC (personal computer)*. If you don't have anyone in-house to do it, you may have to hire someone, but you are usually still better off than sending it outside to be done. The advantages are that great.

That is not to say this project will be easy. It isn't; that's why you need this book. We will be describing the important factors you should consider, first to help you decide if a small computer will improve your accounting system (by easing management decisions), then to help you select a system that fits your needs, and finally to help you through the conversion from your old system to the new computerized system.

The book doesn't provide a fill-in-the-blanks approach or a step-by-step recipe. If this process (decision, selection, setup, and operation) were that straightforward, there would be a lot more than five percent of this country's businesses using computerized accounting by now.

This book presents the steps you will go through in converting to micro-accounting in the order that you should do them. Chapter 1 is an introduction to micro-accounting: what it is, its benefits and weaknesses, and what it will cost you. Chapter 2 helps you decide whether to convert your accounting system at this time by guiding you through a cost/benefit analysis and by offering a set of questions for self-analysis (of your business, not of you). Chapter 3 is a map through the selection and purchasing jungle. Chapter 4 guides you through the conversion process, from scheduling and planning to the final verifications. Chapter 5 covers operating procedures appropriate for computerized systems. Chapter 6 takes a peek ahead.

I.b WHY BOTHER?

You may be asking yourself why you should go through this effort. Why bother computerizing if your present accounting system is working? If your company is growing, a computer can handle that growth much better than a manual system. Once your computerized system is set up, it will be able to handle many times the starting volume with little impact on your overhead. If there are areas of your business where you should see more information, or see the information much sooner, a computer can do that for you.

With a computerized system, you can see a summary status of your business, or any fine detail, at any time.

The computerized system also saves on repetitive tasks. Any billing or payments that are made on a regular monthly basis will be done by pushing a couple of keys on the keyboard. Information on all of your repeat vendors and customers are stored within the system; then, all of your forms (such as purchase orders, sales orders, invoices, and statements) are automatically produced.

A third area where the computer helps is with management reports and analysis. The accounting systems offer varying degrees of sales analysis and vendor performance analysis, for example.

I.c HOW TO USE THIS BOOK

First, notice that the first usage of each glossary word is printed in *italics*. Second, read the whole book before making any final decision to computerize and before taking any action. There are important areas covered in the later chapters that may influence your initial decisions. It was just impossible to cover everything important in the first chapter.

The following is one possible approach for using the information in this book.

1. After the first reading, go back and reread Sections 1.2 through 1.4, noting the items relevant to your situation. You will use this information in steps 3 and 4 below.
2. Read Section 2.1b and make a preliminary decision among:
   a. single-user PC without *hard disk*
   b. single-user PC with hard disk
   c. multi-user micro with hard disk
3. Go through the cost/benefit analysis in Section 2.1c and see if it indicates any further pursuit of micro-accounting.
4. If so, copy Figures 3.6 through 3.10 and use them with Section 3.5 to analyze and list your basic accounting needs. Add any special requirements not listed.

5. At this point you must decide whether you will use the help of a consultant. We recommend you do, because learning about these computerized accounting systems is largely through trial and error. Someone who has been through the process and who knows accounting is almost a necessity for a successful and complete implementation. It is such a struggle to learn on your own that many have tried and given up in frustration. (See Section 3.1).

6. Without a consultant, use your lists of *accounting* needs to shop for accounting *software*. Only after you have selected the software should you choose a brand of *hardware* for your system.

After you have acquired your system, use Chapter 4 to plan and carry out your conversion and Chapter 5 for developing operating procedures.

The Text Bibliography (Appendix B) provides the names of some additional references. These may prove useful if you plan to use the computer for other applications in addition to accounting or wish to delve deeper into microcomputer hardware. The Software Bibliography (Appendix D) provides the names of the major vendors of accounting software for microcomputers and of their related application programs.

7. With a consultant, you can expect guidance and advice for the selection, conversion, and procedures. You may not need to refer again to Chapters 3, 4, or 5, unless you have reason to question something the consultant is doing.

I.d DISCLAIMERS

There are dozens of brands of accounting software on the market, and we have found that the quality varies greatly, not always in relation to price. Several brands have been used to illustrate points throughout the book. These are brands that we have thoroughly evaluated and used, but they still may not be appropriate for every situation. None is perfect, and the weak areas may not be apparent from the scattered references in this book. You will need to do an analysis for your own situation.

The computer hardware used in this book to show

some typical system configurations and costs is not appropriate for every situation. Again, you will need to do an analysis for your own situation.

The methods, formulas, and figures used in this book may not be sufficient or correct for the computerization of your specific accounting system. They will provide examples and guidance but not guarantees.

1

MICRO-ACCOUNTING

1.1 WHAT IS MICRO-ACCOUNTING?

Micro-accounting is keeping your business's books on a microcomputer system, as opposed to using a system of paper *journals* and *ledgers.*

In your manual accounting system, you assign each *financial transaction* to the appropriate *accounts* and record it into the appropriate journals. Later, you manually *post* to the ledger the summary amounts from each journal. Your computerized system does it the same way. You accumulate the information for several financial transactions, then enter that information into the computer, assigning the appropriate *account numbers* and selecting the appropriate journals. Usually, you must tell the computer when to post the journals to the ledger; after that point, the transaction information cannot be altered. You can print these journals and the ledger onto paper at any time, or you can just look at them on the computer's display screen. So the input is basically like the manual system; it is the automatic processing, the automatic reporting, and the great capacity that make all the difference.

Numerous *microcomputer* accounting systems are

being sold today as off-the-shelf software packages. The better ones are designed to work in many different business situations; during the installation you set up parameters and make decisions that result in a system that fits your situation. Additionally, these software packages are divided into mix and match *modules*, so you can select just those accounting functions that are appropriate for your needs. Most of these accounting programs run on many different brands of microcomputers, but sometimes a set of modules will only run on one brand of microcomputer.

The standard modules are *general ledger, accounts receivable, accounts payable,* and *payroll.* Inventory is sometimes offered as well. We will limit our discussions to the standard four modules. Inventory is a complex subject and requires a book of its own.

Specialized programs for certain industries are also available: job costing for the construction industry, time and billing for lawyers and *CPAs*, and various property management packages, to list just a few. These specialized packages cost much more than most standard modules and focus on the specialized management needs of that industry. Unfortunately, many of them give the basic accounting functions, such as the general ledger, an inadequate treatment. Caveat emptor.

The General Ledger Module

The general ledger module is the basis of the whole accounting system. All of the financial transactions of a business end up in the general ledger (or they should, anyway). The sources of the transactions include sales to customers, purchases from vendors, paychecks to employees, and various accounting adjustments (such as for *depreciation* and *amortization*). These different types of transactions are recorded into their respective journals, and summary totals from the journals are periodically posted to the general ledger (Figure 1.1).

When all of the journals have been posted to the general ledger, it becomes a historical record of all of the financial activity of the company. At this point financial

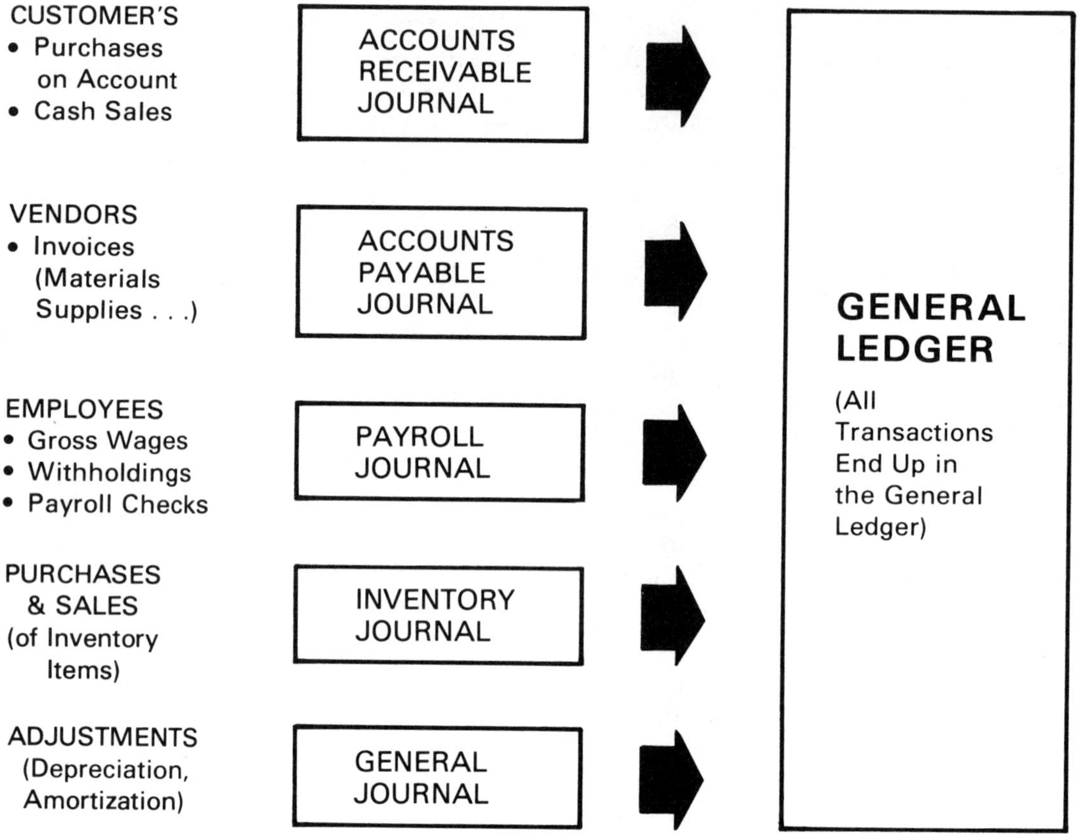

FIGURE 1.1 Accounting System Flow

reports are generated, further summarizing and grouping the information as appropriate for the management decisions of that company. The standard reports are the *balance sheet* and the *income statement* (also called the profit and loss statement). These two reports are dependent upon each other, and together they are called the company's financial statements. There is a third standard financial statement, called the *statement of changes in financial position*, which is not always used by small businesses.

The general ledger module is often sufficient by itself for a small business. It can be set up with a number of journals for handling the low-volume aspects of the company. For example, a service business with relatively few purchase transactions can set up a *cash disburse-*

ments journal within its general ledger module; a separate accounts payable module would not be needed for that system until some future date.

The following reports are usually provided by the general ledger module: the *chart of accounts*, a listing of the journals, the *trial balance worksheet*, the general ledger, the balance sheet, and the income statement. There are samples of these reports in Appendix G. The higher-performance accounting systems provide flexibility in formatting the layout of the financial statements and in the generation of additional management reports.

The Accounts Receivable Module

The accounts receivable module is called for when your customers are generating large numbers of sales transactions—several dozen or more each month. This can mean that you have a large number of customers or that you have a few customers who are generating many sales. The accounts receivable module can help you improve your cash flow and your credit policies. You will use the information it provides to decide which customers deserve credit and to decide when to call a customer about a bill that is growing old. It will maintain a customer list for you, including such information as contacts and phone numbers, the billing cycle you assign to each, their credit rating, their payment history, and much more. A set of mailing labels can usually be printed from the customer list.

When a product is shipped or a service rendered, the information is entered into the system to create a receivable, reflecting a payment owed to you. Some accounts receivable modules will automatically generate an invoice to send at this point. Each receivable and payment from a specific customer is *tracked* and *reconciled*. You can print *statements* for that customer's special billing cycle, monthly, or at any time, and still keep track of the age of each receivable and of each customer's overall status. Discounts and penalties are automatically applied as appropriate or can be overridden.

The accounts receivable module will provide you with

some special reports, notably the *customer ledger*, the *aged receivables report*, and the *overdue receivables report*. These can usually be run for a range of customers, of dates, or of dollar amounts.

The Accounts Payable Module

The accounts payable module is to handle your purchases from the vendors supplying goods and services to your business. It usually prints checks to vendors. It will help you to not pay too soon, yet to receive the desirable discounts. It will ease recurring payments and the accounting for them. You will not be able to double pay the same bill. You will be able to see what you owe at any time, so you can make informed purchasing decisions.

This module will maintain a vendor list with such information as addresses, contacts, telephone numbers, and your salesperson. The special reports available here include a *cash requirements report*, an *aged payables report*, *vendor ledgers*, and possibly a *future payments due report*. Mailing labels are usually printed, and some programs compute commissions paid.

The Payroll Module

The payroll module, as you might suspect, prints the paychecks for your employees, withholding the many different amounts required by the various government agencies, employee benefit plans, and so on. An employee list is maintained, and there are reports on what has been paid and on all of the various withholdings.

While it sounds simple, it is the area least suited for an in-house computer. It is an area with frequent changes, both from employee turnover and status changes and from the periodic changes in the many tax withholding tables involved. It is a sensitive area on two sides: reports to the IRS and the expectations of the employees. Mistakes to either are not taken lightly. The outside payroll services, such as those offered by banks, are competitive to the in-house preparation of most small to medium payrolls.

There is also a type of computer program called after-the-fact payroll; this type of program is designed only to accumulate the payroll records of the company. It does not calculate withholdings or print checks. This would be appropriate for a business that is doing a small payroll manually and only needs aid in the accumulation of the records.

There is a new type of payroll service now, attractive to businesses already using PCs, in which their PCs can be directly linked to their bank's large computer. Employee information is supplied when the service is first engaged. Then, each pay period the payroll information is entered into the PC, which sends it to the bank's computer. That computer computes the proper payments and withholdings for each employee and sends the information back to the PC.

Synopsis

You can usually run these different modules either individually or as an integrated system. They need to run individually in case you only require a single function, accounts payable, for example. But they can be set up to work together in certain ways. The general ledger can automatically post figures from the other modules, treating each module as an additional individual journal. Usually these are period-to-date summary figures for each account, but some systems allow you the option of transferring all of the transaction details from the submodule into the general ledger.

Some of the systems allow you to set up several accounts receivable and/or accounts payable *control accounts* in your general ledger. This would be required by certain types of businesses. For example, a property management company managing three office buildings may prefer to maintain three accounts receivable journals, one for each building. In that case the accounts receivable must be able to handle three different accounts receivable control accounts; then, each building's accounts receivable journal can post into the general ledger separately and be reported separately. For accounts payable, it is a similar need for separate tracking that requires multiple accounts payable journals. A publisher, for example, might have such a need in order to track royalty payments separately from trade expenses.

There are generally two classes of micro-accounting software: low-end and high-end markets. The low-end market offers all four basic accounting modules for about $400 or $500. The high-end market offers the modules separately, at about $500 to $1,000 per module.

The low-end packages are generally very limited in flexibility, capacity, and features. They are appropriate for very small—maybe a million dollars in annual revenues—no-growth situations, where the business can fit into the constraints of the program. Their installation and conversion are not significantly easier than the high-end packages'.

The high-end packages offer more. Their flexibility and features are not mere bells and whistles. They provide you with the ability to tailor your system to your situation and allow the system to grow with your business. An indication of their capabilities is shown by the increasing number of companies that are transferring their accounting from minicomputers (see Table 1.8) onto this type of micro-accounting system. On the other hand, there is a lot of variation in the programs; not all of the high-end packages deserve their high prices.

1.2 WHAT IT CAN DO FOR YOU

The basic purpose of your accounting system is to accurately record all of your financial transactions and report on that data in a useful way. A computer allows you to record more data, in greater detail, than a manual system. Today's microcomputer systems can have nearly unlimited storage capacity; what finally happens is that when too much data is accumulated, the processing time becomes unbearably long. When that time comes, you can add additional microcomputers to distribute your workload, using a *local area network*. This is a mechanism that links your PCs together so they can all share your stored data.

But your accounting system should do more than just store all of that data for you. You want it organized and summarized in ways that are most useful to you: by date, by transaction category, by department. In most manual systems, you determine the organization by the account numbers you assign as you enter transactions into the system. It is no different with the computerized system. As each transaction is entered, the appropriate account numbers have to be assigned. The advantage of the computerized system is that the organization can be much more complex and detailed without adding to the workload of the user. A manual system with a complex chart of accounts and many journals is very cumbersome, slow, and error-prone. The same system on a computer is not much different, operationally, than one with a simple chart of accounts and few journals.

All of the arithmetic involved in grouping and consolidating the data is done automatically, regardless of the complexity of the structure you have set up. It will take the computer longer for more complex systems, but it will still be far faster and more accurate than doing it manually.

The computer allows you to have your cake and eat it, too. You can set up the system to keep very detailed records, but have the normal reports be simple and concise. Whenever you want to look into some aspect in greater detail, that specific information can be produced quickly and easily. This way, the computer system doesn't pour out voluminous reports that swamp you with excessive detail, yet it is all stored there in the system for when you do need it.

All of the better systems allow users to design some of the reports that will come from the system. This means that if you want your financial statements formatted a certain way or emphasizing certain areas, you can have them that way. Some systems allow you to make up several formats for each of those statements so you can tailor them differently for different purposes. With some systems you can design other reports in addition to the standard financial statements. They allow various summing, difference, and percentage arithmetic to be set up between columns and rows of the report. Also, you can select between current period, previous period, year-to-date, budget, and last year's figures for each column.

With a computerized system, you can look at the period's activity for any one account, customer, or vendor. This information can be brought up to the computer's display screen and, if desired, can then be printed out on paper.

The computer system can make a difference in your cash flow. It allows you to keep very close track of your receivables and payables, sometimes including future amounts due and owed. You can set up each of your vendors and customers with a different billing cycle, and you can then make exceptions whenever desired. The computer can check your customers' new orders against their credit records and credit limits automatically, and notify you whenever one exceeds the limit you have set.

Your system will be highly structured, because a computer requires consistency and accurate inputs. Each transaction will be entered the same way. Most programs ask for the date, account number, amount, reference number, and description. Happily, they also provide *default entries* for most of those items, by offering the previous entry for that item. You can then accept it without reentering it, if appropriate, or you can change it as needed. Once the amounts are correctly entered into the system, there is little chance of a processing error, so there is always heavy emphasis placed on the data input procedures. When these procedures are followed, your system will have an extremely low error rate.

The computer will also tell you when your books are about to become out-of-balance, and some will refuse to allow you to continue until you correct that situation. While some people feel that this limits their options, it is a valuable feature because it forces the operator to find the error at the point where it is easiest to find. Once your complex system gets out-of-balance, it is harder for someone to go in and track down the source of the error.

Another powerful function of a computerized system is the automatic printing of your reports, checks, invoices, and statements. This eliminates having to manually type all of those pages and, for high volumes of reports, will increase your accuracy and efficiency many times over. For low volumes the increased accuracy remains, but efficiency falls off because of the setup times involved. It is a lot of work to print just one or two checks using the computer, unless that is the only function it is ever used for.

Once some information is in the system, it will be used over and over. For example, once your customers' names and addresses have been entered into the accounts receivable system, they will be used to send a statement every month automatically. When an established customer places a new order, just entering a short customer number brings up all of the information on that customer for the order entry operator. This can include a credit history and rating, purchase history, payment history, and even pages of any desired comments you care to store on that customer.

One of the most prized aspects of a computerized system is the timeliness of its reports. If the data is input regularly, then up-to-date information about your company's financial status is available at any time, not just at the end of each accounting period. You can know what you owe and what is due to you. Even the *end-of-period processing* is shortened; the completed reports can be ready in days instead of weeks.

1.3 WHAT ITS LIMITATIONS ARE

Capacity

The clearest limitation of a microcomputer system is capacity. While the storage space for data can be extremely large, if you continue increasing it, the *processor* can become overloaded. The data can all be in there, but the computer may not be fast enough to process all of it at a reasonable rate. At that point, the computer begins to take inordinate amounts of time to accomplish its tasks. A system overload can also occur from too much input or output. Even though the processor may not be bogged down, there may not be enough hours in the workday to enter all of the data into the system or to print out all of the reports. The solution to these situations is to add additional computing power—either processors, input terminals, or faster printers—as needed. But this escalates your costs very rapidly (see Chapter 3).

Program Design Parameters

Another set of limitations are the constraints designed into the programs. Someone decided before the programs were written how many digits the largest dollar amount would be, how much room to allow for each customer name, each account number, and so on, for every parameter in the program. Some general ledger programs limit the number of accounts possible in the chart of accounts or the number possible in each category, such as assets or liabilities. These limitations must be avoided satisfactorily during the selection of the system, because they cannot be changed.

Reliability

Computers are no more fragile than your television or stereo equipment, but because they cost more and are used for much more important functions, their reliability is an issue. If you are using a computer for some of your important business operations, and it stops working suddenly, you may be in a lot more trouble than just the repair costs. Just as it took you months to convert your operations onto the computer, you cannot quickly convert back to doing them manually. Suddenly, the question is, "How long can you go without the computer up and running?" A few hours or days, perhaps, but certainly not very long. There are ways of anticipating this problem and easing its impact, such as purchasing a *maintenance contract.* It should not be ignored.

Security

Security is another area where computers are weak. We divide security into three areas: *system security, data security,* and *accounting security.*

System security is concerned with preventing unauthorized use of the computerized accounting system. Without such protection, your accounting information is subject to whims, accidents, or sabotage from many sources. A small business often wants to use its one computer for other functions besides accounting. This greatly increases the exposure of the system because there is a greater chance that some of the users will be experienced at using the computer's *operating system.* This means they can work at a level below that of the accounting system in the computer and can access your accounting *files* directly—completely bypassing any *passwords* built into the accounting system. The way the accounting information is stored in the files varies. Some of the accounting programs make it easy to look at, change, or erase information; others require more expertise.

If the accounting system is all on *floppy diskettes,* and a secure diskette library system has been set up to control their use, then the system is fairly secure. But increasing numbers of businesses are buying hard disks on which to store their data. A hard disk can hold the equivalent of dozens of floppy diskettes, and the information is stored in the computer at all times. Thus, all of the users have access to all of the data in the computer, if they have learned enough about that particular computer's operating system. If you think that is far-fetched, consider the MS/DOS operating system used on the popular IBM personal computers. There are already hundreds of thousands of IBM PC users who have learned to use MS/DOS to some degree. The MS/DOS diskette and instruction manual can be purchased from numerous computer stores for just $60, and it will work on any IBM PC or XT, including yours.

One of the basic principles of accounting is the separation of certain accounting functions so that if something is done wrong in one area, it cannot be easily covered up throughout the system. For example, the same person who adds or removes employees should not generate the paychecks. The person who places orders with vendors should not handle the receipt of the goods when they arrive, and the person taking orders from customers should not handle the checks sent in payment. A computerized system can result in fewer people involved in accounting operations, so special attention must be paid to this idea of separation of duties when the system is set up.

One way to separate various functions is to assign a different *password* to each function. Only those operators assigned to a particular function should know the password for using it. If your business is not large enough to have such separation, the passwords need not be implemented; however, other controls should be instituted (see Chapter 5).

Data security is concerned with the fragility of the accounting data. An electrical surge on the power line, a blow to the hard disk while you are writing to it, or a drink spilled on a diskette—these and many other everyday occurrences can destroy your company's computerized records instantaneously. There are preventative measures to deal with this problem (see Chapter 5), but it must be listed as one of the computer's weak points.

Accounting security has to do with the *audit trails*, trails of documents that link the system inputs to the final figures reported by the system. These are a function of the accounting program design and are weak in most micro systems (and nonexistent in some).

Selection

Another weak point in microcomputer accounting systems is the difficulty of selecting one that is right for you. There are somewhere between 50 and 300 accounting software packages on the market, and new ones are appearing every week. While there are some fairly good systems out there, we have also seen some fairly poor ones. The real problem is not merely the quantity or quality, but the complexity of the product. The difficulty of evaluating even a single system, relative to your needs, is overwhelming. So far, no one has come up with a good solution to this problem (see Chapter 3).

Setup

The final problem about these accounting systems is that none of them are easy to set up. The easiest ones are those in which everything is already fixed, so that all you have to do is adjust to fit their system and enter your beginning balances into their chart of accounts. The best systems are extremely flexible, so they can be adjusted to fit your requirements. But that means that the setup requires more decisions, often requiring both accounting and computer expertise. This book will help you with these areas.

1.4 WHAT ARE THE COSTS?

The obvious costs of a computerized accounting system are the costs of the computer hardware and software (equipment and programs). We will cover these, but first we will discuss some of the hidden costs.

Research and Selection

The effort you and your staff put into selecting your system can be a large cost. This includes the analysis of your current system and the definition of your needs, followed by the analysis of the prospective systems. Selecting the software is much more difficult than selecting the hardware, and accounting software is the most complex and expensive kind.

Using an experienced **independent** consultant who knows the better brands of accounting software is usually more cost-effective than struggling through it yourself. The results are likely to be both faster and better. The consultant can quickly guide you through the maze to your goal, without the searching and learning you would have to go through. Such a consultant will cost you from $50 to $100 per hour, depending on his/her background in business, computers, and accounting.

By looking at your financial statements and discussing your business methods, the consultant should be able to learn enough about your current system in a couple of hours, unless your needs are exceptional, to be able to recommend one or two systems. Demonstrations of these recommended systems should not cost you anything if you can find a dealer that carries both the hardware and software that you are interested in. However, if you want your knowledgeable consultant to give the demonstrations, that will cost you a few more hours.

People and Space

There are some costs involved in preparing space, furniture, and staff for the transition. While special rooms or furniture are not required, you should consider the uses the computer will be put to.

If one person is going to sit at the computer all day long, the chair should provide that person adequate support and comfort; discomfort can result in both health problems and slow work. The keyboard is easiest to use if it is placed a few inches below the normal table height. Most typing tables are lowered in that way and can be used for some of the smaller computer terminals or personal computers. The lighting is an important factor in the placement of the input terminals. A light or window behind the operator will reflect off the display screen into the operators' eyes, causing discomfort and slowing the work. The best lighting is provided by a ceiling light directly over the input keyboard.

Some types of printers are quite noisy and should not be placed in an area where people are working or talking on the telephone. On the other hand, the printer needs to be close to the PC, or else the operator will be constantly walking back and forth between the two machines. Often the only solution is to buy an acoustical enclosure for the noisy printer. These are soundproof boxes that cover the printer and have a hinged lid. They range from $200 to over $500.

The staff that will be using the computer, and all those who will be receiving reports from it, should be involved early. This can be in the form of meetings, discussion groups, and formal training. Introductory courses and interactive tutorial programs are available at most computer stores and cost from $50 to $200. You can find introductory books on specific types of computers at the stores that sell that brand. Training on your specific accounting software will probably require bringing in a specialist at $40 to $80 per hour.

Supplies and Forms

You will need to acquire a store of computer supplies necessary for the operation of the computer. These supplies include blank diskettes, printer ribbons and paper, and any special forms needed by the accounting system. Diskettes cost from $25 to $60 for a box of 10, depending on the quality and type. Printer ribbons vary from $3 to $30, depending on the brand. Special forms might include checks, invoices, and statements; most often the accounting software manual explains what forms are needed and where to get them. You may want to print up special forms with your company name on them. We recommend waiting until the system is running smoothly before ordering any special forms.

The Conversion

Then there is the *conversion process* itself, involving preparation and gathering of data, setting up the chart of accounts, designing the various reports, and keying in all of the initial data. This last might include a beginning balance and 12 budget figures for each account, your customer and vendor lists, and all of the information for each entry. This generally takes weeks, and the help of a consultant can run you over $1,000 per module.

Maintenance

The maintenance of your computer equipment can be handled as a per-hour repair charge or on a service contract basis. The hourly repair rates are from $40 to $75 per hour, and some equipment (hard disks) will have to be sent to the factory for any repairs. The service contract is similar to insurance. You pay a fixed amount monthly or annually, and any problems are fixed without additional charge. Such contracts run from 10 to 20 percent of your purchase price per year, depending on which company you contract with and the level of service you select. On-site, 24-hour guaranteed repairs will cost you much more than carry-in, 3-day guaranteed repairs. Table 1.1 shows some typical service contract prices charged by IBM and by MAI/Sorbus for IBM PC components.

Hardware and Software

The cost of computer hardware depends on the brand, system size, and on what types of accessories you buy. We have priced several representative microcomputer systems, ranging from a low-end business system to some larger multi-user systems, to give you a very general idea of a system's total price (see Tables 1.3 through 1.7). As you can see, the prices rise rapidly as you expand the capabilities of the systems. But it is all relative. Just for perspective, Table 1.8 shows some cost figures for a *minicomputer* (the next size up from microcomputers); these are for the IBM System/36, a fairly new, small minicomputer that is representative of the prices at that level.

TABLE 1-1

Hardware Maintenance: Typical Annual Charges

January 1984 *Compiled by Knight & Company, CPAs*

	IBM			MAI/Sorbus	
Item	*On-Site*	*Pkup +Del*	*Carry -In*	*On-Site*	*Carry -In*
Computer:					
IBM PC CPU	165	132	106	180	108
IBM XT CPU	275	220	175	222	141
Keyboard	incl.				
Screen, monochrome	44	35	28	60	36
Screen, color	125	100	80	120	75
Screen, graphics	incl.				
Storage, diskettes	83	67	54	84	51
Storage, IBM XT hard disk	295	235	190	294	189
Printer—IBM PC printer	63	50	40	144	87
Printer—Epson MX100				180	108
Printer—TI 855					
Printer—Okidata ML93				300	192
Printer—IBM/NEC 3550				366	256
Printer—NEC 5500/7700 series				396	252
Modem—Hayes Smartmodem 300				60	36

Accounting systems require only basic computer components: the processing unit and storage, input keyboard, display screen, and a printer. Most *micros* come with the first four items, and the printer is optional. This is not because you don't need one; it is because there are so many options available for printing. The system manufacturers know they can't predict what you want, so they leave that choice up to you. Table 1.2 is a list of two representative lines of printers. Notice that the *letter-quality printers* are both slower and more expensive than the *dot matrix printers.* (Types of printers are discussed in Section 3.6.)

All of the PC systems we show here use the MS/DOS operating system. Much of the accounting software runs on both the CP/M and the MS/DOS operating systems. CP/M is a much older product and runs on processors with less capacity. Few new programs are being written for it, and it

TABLE 1-2

Two Representative Printer Lines

MODEL	MAXIMUM SPEED	PAPER WIDTH	LQ?*	NLQ?*	C?*	APPROXIMATE LIST PRICE (4/84)
Okidata Corporation:						
ML-80	80 CPS*	9.5″	N	N	Y	$ 450
ML-82A	120	9.5	N	N	Y	550
ML-83A	120	16	N	N	Y	900
ML-92	160	9.5	N	Y	Y	700
ML-93	160	16	N	Y	Y	1,250
ML-84	200	16	N	Y	Y	1,400
P-2350	350	16	N	N	Y	2,550
P-2410	350	16	N	Y	Y	2,850
NEC Information Systems:						
8023	100	9.5	N	N	Y	$ 800
2000	20	16	Y	N	N	1,150
3500/3550	33	16	Y	N	N	2,300+250**
7700	55	16	Y	N	N	3,100+250**

*CPS = *characters per second*
LQ = *letter-quality characters*
NLQ = *near-letter-quality characters*
C = *compressed characters possible*

***(The additional $250 on the last two printers is for a necessary option called a tractor feed.)*

is not capable of running many of the powerful new programs recently released. MS/DOS is the most popular operating system for new programs for PCs. At the next level up, multi-user micros, there are several versions of the UNIX operating system vying for the lead spot.

Our first representative system (Table 1.3) is a portable PC with a dot matrix printer. The next system (Table 1.4) is a standard PC system, but with twice the storage capacity, additional accounting modules, and a faster printer. Both of these systems are floppy diskette based; thus, their storage capacities are so small that they are only appropriate for the smallest of businesses. On these systems your accounting programs and data will all reside on diskettes. With some accounting systems, you end up with six or seven diskettes for each module you are using plus *backup* copies of all of them, and sometimes they require a whole new set each month. You can begin to feel like the diskettes are taking over the whole place, multiplying out of control. On the other hand, some of the programs, such as CYMA, have only one *program diskette* and one or two *data diskettes* per accounting module.

TABLE 1-3

Representative Systems' Costs
Dual Diskette Portable

DESCRIPTION	APPROXIMATE LIST PRICE (4/84)	MANUFACTURER
COMPUTER: Chameleon	$2,000	Seequa Computer Corp.
Some compatibility to IBM PC		
128K memory		
Dual 160K floppy drives		
High-resolution AN display		
MS/DOS operating system		
PerfectWriter word processing		
PerfectCalc spreadsheet		
PRINTER: Okidata ML-82A	550	Okidata Corporation
SUPPLIES:	200	
diskettes		
printer ribbons		
computer paper		
SOFTWARE: CYMA G/L	750	CYMA Corporation
CONSULTING:		
Selection	150	
Accounting installation	1,500 to 2,500, depending on the shape and complexity of your system.	
Total	$5,000 to 6,000	
ANNUAL:		
Maintenance contracts:		
computer carry-in	200	
printer carry-in	100	
Insurance (normal office policies do not cover computers)	75	

TABLE 1-4

Representative Systems' Costs
Dual Diskette PC

DESCRIPTION	APPROXIMATE LIST PRICE (4/84)	MANUFACTURER
COMPUTER: IBM PC 64K memory Dual 360K floppy drives High-resolution AN display	$3,300	IBM Corporation
PRINTER: Okidata ML-84	1,400	Okidata Corporation
SUPPLIES: diskettes printer ribbons computer paper	300	
SOFTWARE: CYMA G/L, A/R	1,500	CYMA Corporation
PC/DOS 2.0 operating system	60	IBM Corporation
CONSULTING:		
Selection	200	
Accounting installation	2,500 to 3,500, depending on the shape and complexity of your system.	
Total	$9,500 to 10,500	
ANNUAL:		
Maintenance contracts:		
computer carry-in	350	
printer carry-in	150	
Insurance (normal office policies do not cover computers)	150	

CYMA also takes up relatively little storage space per account and transaction.

With the next system (Table 1.5), the main differences are a great increase in the storage space available, a different set of accounting programs, and the substitution of a fast letter-quality printer. Your storage needs are determined by your current volumes of accounting transactions, your growth projections, and the other programs you will be running on your PC. The choice of the expensive printer is not necessary. That would depend on the type of printing your situation demands (covered in Section 3.6) and on your budget. This printer is slower than the dot matrix printer from the last system, but not as slow as the CPS (characters per second) numbers might lead you to assume; it goes through any *white space* (where no characters are to be printed) on a report much faster.

The next two systems (Tables 1.6 and 1.7) illustrate

TABLE 1-5

Representative Systems' Costs
10MB Hard Disk PC

DESCRIPTION	APPROXIMATE LIST PRICE (4/84)	MANUFACTURER
COMPUTER: IBM XT	$5,900	IBM Corporation
256K memory		
Single 360K floppy drive		
10MB Hard disk drive		
High-resolution AN display		
PRINTER: NEC 7730	3,100	NEC Information Systems
SUPPLIES:	400	
diskettes		
printer ribbons		
computer paper & forms		
SOFTWARE: Solomon III G/L, A/R, A/P, PR	2,400	Computech Group, Inc.
PC/DOS 2.0 operating system	60	IBM Corporation
CONSULTING:		
Selection	300	
Accounting installation	3,500 to 5,000, depending on the shape and complexity of your system.	
Total	$15,500 to 17,000	
ANNUAL:		
Maintenance contracts:		
computer on-site	700	
printer on-site	400	
Insurance (normal office policies do not cover computers)	200	

TABLE 1-6

Representative Systems' Costs
PC network, 4 workstations, 2 printers

DESCRIPTION	APPROXIMATE LIST PRICE (4/84)	MANUFACTURER
COMPUTERS:		
4 IBM PCs	$14,000	IBM Corporation
128K memory		
Dual 360K floppy drives		
High-resolution AN display		
32MB hard disk (external)	3,000	Davong Systems
Power conditioner	100	Panamax
NETWORKING:		
4 PCNET circuit cards + software	2,900	Orchid Technology
4 Cables	100	
PRINTERS:		
Okidata ML-84	1,400	Okidata Corporation
NEC 7730	3,100	NEC Information Systems
SUPPLIES:	450	
diskettes		
printer ribbons		
computer paper & forms		
SOFTWARE: CYMA G/L, A/R, A/P, PR	2,500	CYMA Corporation
PC/DOS 2.0 operating system	60	IBM Corporation
CONSULTING:		
Selection	400	
Accounting installation	5,000 to 7,000, depending on the shape and complexity of your system.	
Total	$33,000 to 35,000	
ANNUAL:		
Maintenance contracts:		
computer on-site	1,500	
printers on-site	700	
Insurance (normal office policies do not cover computers)	500	

how the costs of a PC network differ from those of a multi-user micro. The main reason for spending so much more for a network is that it can be built up over time, whereas the Altos has to be purchased all at once. Either of these systems would be a large project to implement for a business that has never had an in-house computer before.

The cost of software varies by brand and does not always reflect the relative value. We have evaluated most

TABLE 1-7

Representative Systems' Costs
Multi-user computer, 4 workstations, 2 printers

DESCRIPTION	APPROXIMATE LIST PRICE (4/84)	MANUFACTURER
COMPUTER:		
Altos 586	$11,000	Altos Corporation
512K memory		
Single 1MB floppy drive		
32MB Hard disk drive		
4 WY-50 workstations	4,000	Wyse Technology
Power conditioner	100	Panamax
PRINTERS:		
Okidata ML-84	1,400	Okidata Corporation
NEC 7730	3,100	NEC Information Systems
SUPPLIES:	450	
diskettes		
printer ribbons		
computer paper & forms		
SOFTWARE:		
Operating system: XENIX	1,000	Altos Corporation
Language: COBOL	400	RealWorld Corp.
Accounting: RealWorld (MBSI)	2,600	RealWorld Corp.
GL, AR, AP, PR		
CONSULTING:		
Selection	250	
Accounting installation	5,000 to 7,000, depending on the shape and complexity of your system.	
Total	$29,000 to 31,000	
ANNUAL:		
Maintenance contracts:		
computer on-site	2,500	
printers on-site	700	
Insurance (normal office policies do not cover computers)	500	

TABLE 1-8

Representative Systems' Costs
Small Minicomputer

DESCRIPTION	APPROXIMATE LIST PRICE (1/84)	MANUFACTURER
Two-user System/36: computer 128K memory 60MB hard disk storage diskette magazine 240 LPM printer 2 IBM 5291 displays system support programs RPG II compiler utilities programs	$49,836	IBM Corporation
Three-user System/36: computer 256K memory 200MB hard disk storage diskette magazine 240 LPM printer 3 IBM 5291 displays system support programs RPG II compiler utilities programs	$64,336	IBM Corporation
SUPPLIES: diskettes printer ribbons computer paper & forms	???*	
SOFTWARE:	$2,000 and way up, per accounting module	
CONSULTING:	????*	
Total	$?*	
ANNUAL:		
Maintenance contracts:		
computer on-site	????*	
printers on-site	????*	
Insurance (normal office policies do not cover computers)	????*	

**Not available*

of the accounting software available for micros and can safely say that there are no perfect packages out there. You will just have to look for one that is strong in the areas you need. In Appendix D we have listed many microcomputer accounting packages, along with the addresses and telephone numbers of their vendors.

With word processing or financial analysis programs, you can trade off performance against cost; that is, you may be willing to put up with some inconvenience in order to save on the cost. With accounting software, you should not be willing to give up performance, because it could cost you much more than the few hundred dollars you may save. A good illustration of this point is made by Richard Brock of Informatics General Corporation: He shows you a photograph of a mountain climber dangling high on a cliff, suspended by a single rope, and asks how much price versus performance shopping you think the climber did when purchasing that rope.

Cost Trends

The cost trends of microcomputer systems have been decreasing for years, and they will continue in that direction. The major decreases have been in the prices of memory and storage: These used to make up the largest part of the total system cost. Now that honor can easily rest with the printer, if you want a fast dot matrix or letter-quality printer. Although hard disks are still a couple thousand dollars, their prices are dropping fast.

At times the prices of software seem to be rising, but the value has been rising far faster. What you receive for that higher price is many more features and much more power than just a year ago. The newer programs are being written in more powerful computer languages and for the newer, more powerful operating systems. The differences are immediately obvious when you compare an older program to a newer one, and the improvements are worth the increased prices. One of those newer packages is Solomon III, and it has many innovative features.

2

ASSESSING YOUR NEEDS

2.1 IS A MICRO FOR YOU?

General Considerations

We recommend you approach the question of computerizing in two parts. First, you must determine if your accounting system will benefit from a computer. Then, you have to determine which computer system best fits your needs and whether you can afford it.

That first determination is not based solely on your current accounting bottlenecks. It is also a philosophical and cultural question. Look at how a computer is going to affect the work flow and the communications in your business. Many people will be affected besides the accounting staff who will operate it. It may allow you to institute a budget process or keep separate departmental records for the first time. At first, many people will fear and resist the computer; this is understandable. They may see the new computer as a threat to their jobs, or they may anticipate the discomfort and extra effort that accompanies change.

Consider the history of the automobile. When automobiles were new to most people (right after the turn of the century), a user had to either become an amateur mechanic or hire one full-time as a chauffeur. Many roads were inadequate, having been developed for less sophisticated vehicles, but they were sometimes better than no road at all. Today's drivers take the highway network for granted, and they don't have to know much about their automobiles' engine, transmission, and suspension.

The microcomputer hardware of today is beyond the stage where an expert is needed to operate it (although the automatic transmission is still lacking). But the software can still make your ride rough. Like the early road system, it may or may not get you to your destination without a breakdown or worse. The use of accounting software is not as smooth as the use of *word processing* and *spreadsheet* software, and it is a far longer road to travel.

Perhaps the question of whether to computerize is really more a question of when to make the move. When was the best time to replace a fleet of horse-drawn wagons with mechanized delivery trucks? For some companies, it was as soon as the roads were adequate and the support services (mechanics and spare parts) were available. For others, it was appropriate to wait many years or to mechanize a little at a time.

Some Hardware Lessons

You know your business needs and what direction you want your company to move in better than anyone else. You should have a fairly good idea of the capabilities, limitations, and costs of microcomputers from reading Chapter 1. At this point, if you are still interested in computerizing your accounting, you should go through a cost/benefit analysis. This does not need to be a rigorous exercise; after all, many of the benefits will not have any set value—just whatever value you place on them. Before you can carry out that analysis, you will need to learn some more about microcomputer systems and make a couple of decisions that will affect your costs.

First, you must decide whether you need a *multi-user*

system. Most small businesses start off with a *single-user system*—one computer used by one person at a time, often for many different applications. The multi-user systems not only cost more, but they also require more computer expertise and sophistication from the users. You need one only if you will have several people needing information from one central pool of data at the same time. For example, if you have three people taking orders on an order entry system and several more performing accounting functions on the same data, then you need a multi-user system.

There are a couple of other factors to consider as well. There is much less software to choose from for the multi-user micros, and what there is tends to cost several times as much as the single-user equivalent. There are two major approaches to multi-user systems: a single computer with multiple input stations and a network of single-user computers (see Figure 2.1).

With a single computer, the performance deteriorates as you increase the number of users. With some systems, it

1. A Typical Multi-User Microcomputer System

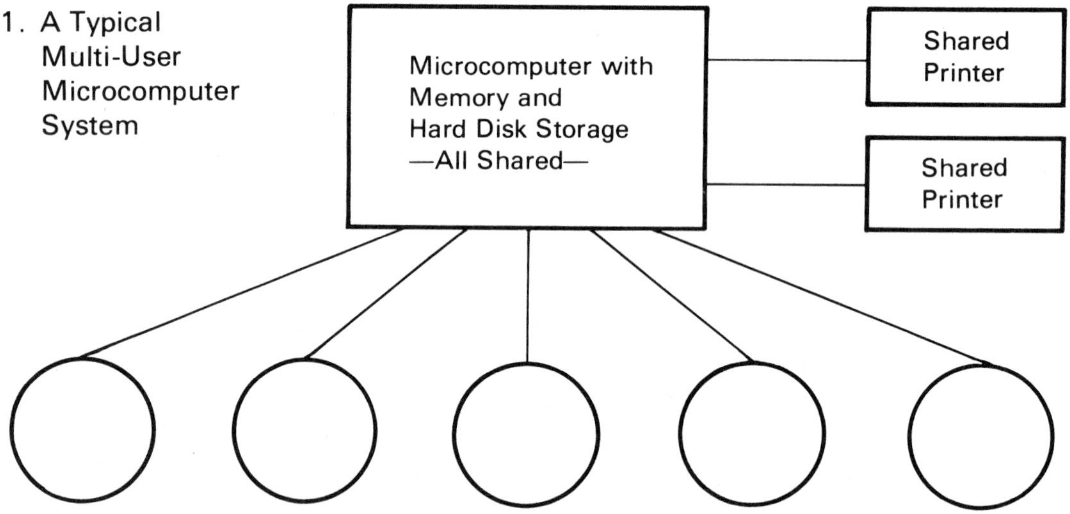

"Dumb terminal" input stations: just a keyboard and a display screen.

Usually any user can use any input station. The computer uses the user-ID numbers to identify users.

FIGURE 2.1 Multi-User versus Local Area Network Systems

2. An Inexpensive Type of Network.

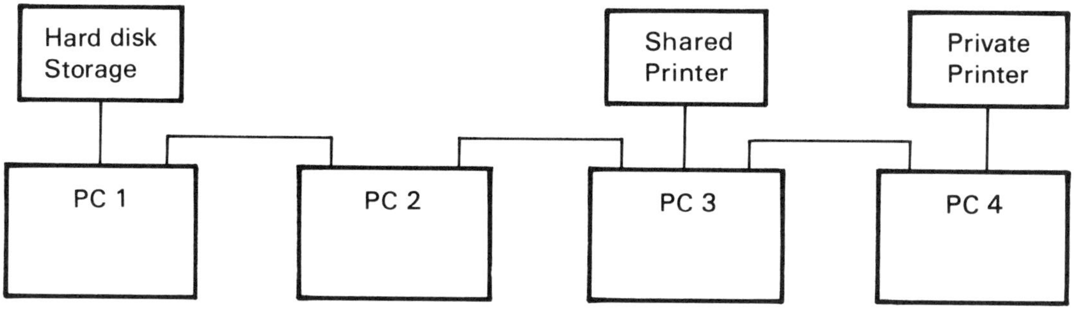

Usually network hard disks can be divided into two parts: private for that PC and shared among all PCs.

3. A Higher-Performance Type of Network.

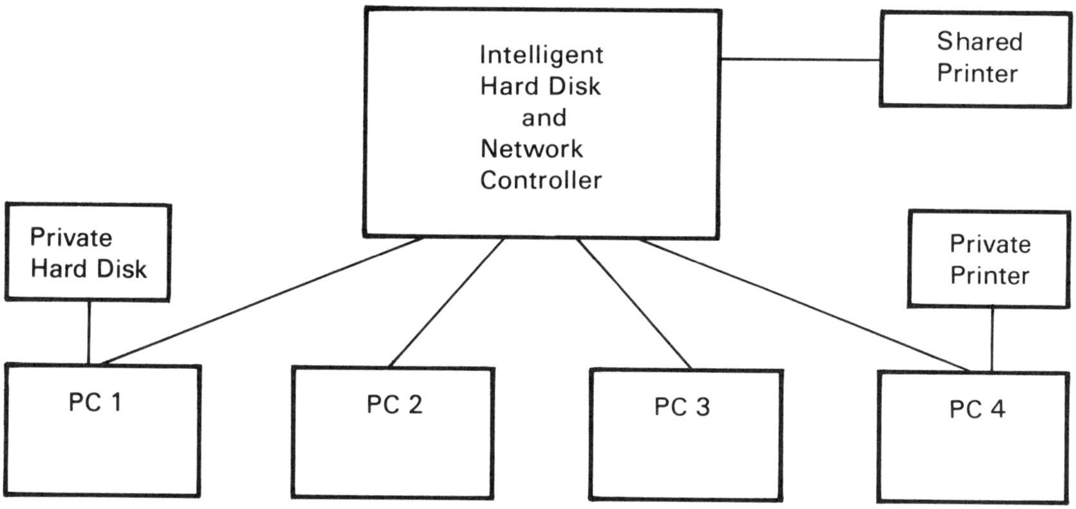

In this type of network, a microcomputer is dedicated to controlling the network. This is a more costly, higher-performance type of network.

FIGURE 2.1 Multi-User versus Local Area Network Systems (con.)

gets intolerable with three users, whereas others can handle more than 16 comfortably. It depends on the computer, the software, and the operations running at that time.

The second type of multi-user system is built by linking together several single-user micros with high-speed communication cables. This is called a local area network (Because the distance between the computers is limited to several thousand feet, all of the computers in the network must be connected with special wiring.). A local area network must share at least one hard disk storage unit so the different PCs can all access the same data.

Each computer's performance does not deteriorate significantly as additional PCs are added to the network; however, waiting lines develop at the shared hard disk because only one PC can use it at a time. Also, most micro software packages are not designed to run on a network, so there may be compatibility problems. Some accounting software vendors are now developing special versions of their programs for certain brands of networks (see Chapter 6).

Cost-wise, the typical multi-user micro starts beating the networked micros at about four users, but networks are increasing in popularity anyway. Many businesses start out with one single-user micro and later add a few more around the office. At that point it may not cost much to convert those micros into a network. Because they have worked up to it gradually, they have also acquired the computer expertise and sophistication needed for either networked or multi-user equipment.

If you decide to go with a single-user system, you then have to decide whether you want or need a hard disk with your system. You will need one if any of your accounting modules will be running a couple hundred transactions per month, if you have several hundred vendors or regular customers, or if you would like to accumulate the transaction details for a whole year instead of for each month separately. Hard disks come in sizes from 5 million bytes to over 100 million bytes; the size you will need depends on both your accounting volume and on what software you select. Some accounting programs use up several times as much room as others, usually because they keep more detailed information. You may or may not need that much detail.

Many business users buy a hard disk even though they

don't need it for the capacity; there are several other advantages gained. Any program that reads the disk storage often (most accounting programs do) will run four to six times faster using a hard disk rather than floppy diskettes. Also, because the hard disk stores all of your programs and data files in the computer all of the time, you would have to deal with floppies only when making backup or archival copies of your accounting data. You wouldn't have dozens of diskettes to keep organized and to exchange into and out of the computer periodically (whenever the computer instructs you to).

Cost/benefit Analysis

We have provided some forms to help with your cost/benefit analysis. The formulas used were developed by the Association of Computer Users (ACU) for the purpose of rough cost/benefit analysis of multipurpose microcomputers.

Complete Figure 2.2, the costs, based on the type of system you decide is appropriate. Use Tables 1.1 through 1.8 as examples of systems and for typical costs. You may need to adjust these costs for your circumstances; for example, you may require a stronger maintenance contract or additional accounting modules. The prices for equipment, software, and maintenance change rapidly, so you may find some differences from what we list here. They should be small in relation to your overall cost figure and will almost certainly lower it. Also note that part 5 of Figure 2.2 should only be completed for those modules that you are bringing in from an outside accounting service.

The one-time costs, such as purchasing the system, installation, and training, must be annualized so you can compare annual costs to annual benefits. You can assume a three-year life for the system for a conservative analysis. This means that dividing the one-time costs by three will yield a rough annual cost sufficient for your comparison.

For the benefits side, use Figure 2.3 for those modules you are converting from manual to micro. Use Figure 2.4 for those modules that you are bringing in from an outside accounting service.

FIGURE 2.2

COST/BENEFIT ANALYSIS (ACCOUNTING ONLY)

Costs

Item	*Estimated Cost*
1. One-time costs:	
a. Computer(s)	$______
b. Printer(s)	______
c. Software	______
d. Furniture	______
e. Computer system training	______
f. Consulting—selection	______
—accounting installation	______
Subtotal	______
2. Divide by three to get annualized cost, assuming a three-year life for the system.	______
3. Annual costs	
a. Supplies	______
b. Maintenance	______
c. Insurance	______
4. Subtotal (2+3)	______

5. If bringing accounting in-house from an outside accounting service, add these additional costs (just for the relevant accounting functions). First there are the additional labor requirements. Enter an estimate of the number of labor-hours it would take per month to manually do that part of your books. Then enter the average cost per hour of your bookkeeping staff.

General ledger:	____ hrs/mo × ____ $/hr × 12mo × 50% =	______
Accts rec:	____ hrs/mo × ____ $/hr × 12mo × 25% =	______
Accts payable:	____ hrs/mo × ____ $/hr × 12mo × 50% =	______
Payroll:	____ hrs/mo × ____ $/hr × 12mo × 25% =	______

There will also be some additional training required. Figure on about one month's staff cost per module (just use the hrs/mo and $/hr figures from above).

FIGURE 2.2 (con.)

COST/BENEFIT ANALYSIS (ACCOUNTING ONLY)

Costs

Item	*Estimated Cost*
General ledger: ____ hrs/mo × ____ $/hr =	________
Accts rec: ____ hrs/mo × ____ $/hr =	________
Accts payable: ____ hrs/mo × ____ $/hr =	________
Payroll: ____ hrs/mo × ____ $/hr =	________
Subtotal	________
6. Divide by three to get annualized cost, assuming a three-year life for the system.	________
7. Total annual cost (lines 4 and 6 if applicable)	________

The benefits include both intangible benefits and formulas for each accounting module and for the overall system. You should assign an annual value to each of those intangibles that apply to your planned system. Then you must come up with your figures for the inputs to the formulas: your annual sales, total annual accounts receivable, average outstanding accounts receivable, and average cost/hour of your bookkeeping help. Finally, estimate the number of hours per month your bookkeeper spends on each of the four accounting functions listed.

When you bring in your accounting from an outside service, you must add some costs and work up the benefits differently. The basic system costs are handled in the same way. Then you project the annual reduction in charges for the outside accounting services as a positive benefit. On the other hand, your new in-house system will require additional in-house labor. This cost is figured by estimating how many labor hours per month would have to be spent to do each accounting function manually in-house, per month, and applying the computerization labor reduction formulas

FIGURE 2.3

COST/BENEFIT ANALYSIS (ACCOUNTING ONLY) BENEFITS—IF CONVERTING FROM MANUAL TO MICRO

	Estimated $ Benefit
1. Overall:	
a. Growth handled smoothly	$________
b. Reports available on a more timely basis	________
c. No more arithmetic mistakes	________
2. General Ledger:	
a. Reduce the general ledger labor requirement:	
____hrs/mo × ____ $/hr × 12mo × 50% =	________
b. Better control of your business:	
– tailored reports—you can target data	________
– summary status of business always available	________
– details of accounts always available	________
– period closings and financial statements available within a week or two	________
– aids in keeping books in balance	________
3. Accounts Receivable:	
a. Improve bad debt ratio by 0.5%	
________________ × 0.05 = Total annual accounts receivable	________
b. Reduce average A/R by 10% (and reinvest)	
________________ × 0.1 × 0.08 = Average accounts receivable interest rate	________
c. Reduce accounts receivable labor requirements	
______ hrs/mo × ______ $/hr × 12mo × 75% =	________
d. You can see detail/history on any customer at any time	________
e. Analysis of who buys what, when, and how they pay	________
4. Accounts Payable:	
a. Reduce accounts payable labor requirements	
______ hrs/mo × ______ $/hr × 12mo × 50% =	________

FIGURE 2.3 (con.)

COST/BENEFIT ANALYSIS (ACCOUNTING ONLY) BENEFITS—IF CONVERTING FROM MANUAL TO MICRO

	Estimated $ Benefit
b. Better cash flow management:	
- see what you owe and when it is due	______
- track the value of discounts lost	______
- see where you stand with each vendor	______
- be able to monitor each bill separately	______
5. Payroll:	
a. Reduce payroll labor requirements	
______ hrs/mo × ______ $/hr × 12mo × 75% =	______
6. Total Annual Benefit	$______

in reverse. For example, if a manual accounts receivable system will be reduced by 75 percent when computerized, then bringing it in-house from a service will require 25 percent of the labor of a wholly manual system.

If you bring your accounting in from outside, you will have to either train some of your staff in bookkeeping or hire someone who knows it. This is one of the hidden costs of converting. Potential users do not always realize that micro-accounting systems require someone with bookkeeping skills to operate them. Estimate a cost equivalent to about one month's staff time for each module. For example, if you would require one full-time person to do your accounts receivable manually, then you would estimate a training cost of one month's salary for that hypothetical person.

Now if you plug those amounts into the relevant formulas and carry out the calculations, you should arrive at the annual figures for each item. Compare the total annual benefits to the total annual costs. If either side is more than about 15 percent greater than the other side, that is a clear indication of whether or not to computerize. If the

FIGURE 2.4

COST/BENEFIT ANALYSIS (ACCOUNTING ONLY)
BENEFITS—IF CONVERTING FROM OUTSIDE SERVICE TO MICRO

	Estimated $ Benefit
1. Overall:	
a. Your business records not sent off premises	
– they remain available	$______
– confidentiality remains under your control	______
b. Reports available on a more timely basis	______
c. Downtime and data losses under your control	______
d. No more telephone/mail/messenger fees	______
2. General Ledger:	
a. Reduction of outside service fees:	
______ $/mo × 12mo	______
3. Accounts receivable:	
a. Reduction of outside service fees:	
______ $/mo × 12mo	______
4. Accounts payable:	
a. Reduction of outside service fees:	
______ $/mo × 12mo	______
5. Payroll:	
a. Reduction of outside service fees:	
______ $/mo × 12mo	______
6. Total Annual Benefits	$______

totals do not differ by at least 15 percent, then further analysis is indicated.

2.2 LOOK AHEAD

When considering your computer and accounting needs, look at the growth possibilities for your business. Your computer system must be chosen with your expansion plans in mind. As long as you can expand your system to handle your volume of transactions, it will ease your growth. It will allow you to forgo hiring additional staff much longer than without the computer. Your procedures will not have to be changed as often.

This means you should plan a path to a multi-user system, even if you will not be needing one for several years. Look at the compatibility of each brand of PC with the networks on the market. Many of the older PCs will not work with any network or will work only with that manufacturer's network (with other PCs of the same brand).

If, instead of building networks, you later decide to upgrade from your PC to a large multi-user microcomputer, you will want to be able to transfer your accumulated accounting data over to the new computer with a minimum of trouble. That will be easier if both computers and their respective operating systems are popular brands that will be supported over the years. This means plenty of specialists will be available to help with the project, and you will not have to pay a premium for that help.

You should also consider the directional changes that might happen to your business over time. You may start up an additional enterprise in the next few years, in which case you would suddenly need a system that could handle multiple companies—many computerized accounting systems don't. Your business might branch into a new area that requires many repeating entries into the books every month. A recurring transaction entry feature would then become important. While you can't predict all such occurrences, you might see some appearing on your horizon.

2.3 ACCOUNTING NEEDS

You will need to determine your accounting needs fairly precisely in order to select a good accounting software package for your situation. Read Sections 3.1 through 3.6, then use Section 3.7 to develop your lists of needs. Your lists should differentiate between minimum requirements and things you would *like* to see. Some of those needs will be new features that your current system does not offer; others will be features that you already have and want to keep.

The best candidates for computerization are those areas that once worked well but have become bottlenecks solely due to the increased volume of your business. Areas that never worked manually will not begin working just because they have been automated. Those parts of your system will have to be redesigned before being computerized.

Be sure to involve an accountant in this project to help with both the determination of your needs and the setup of the new system. It is worth doing right, since you will be relying on the new system for a long time. The accountant who currently works on your books is the best person to help you. However, you should not have to pay for any learning time, for either accountants or consultants. When you are paying for guidance, you expect the guide to know the way.

2.4 HOW SOME OTHERS HAVE DONE IT

In this section you will see what some businesses went through to achieve their micro-accounting systems. All of these conversions actually took place, although names and dates have been changed to protect the innocent. The costs and the durations are accurate. Note that none of these companies did a cost/benefit analysis to decide whether to computerize; instead, they all had used or heard about others who used microcomputers, and saw the potential for their own situations. None of them were fully aware of all of the possible pitfalls. They did know they were taking a chance, just as with any business decision.

ABC Manufacturing

Who did it:	Experienced bookkeeper
Accounting needs:	Typical—GL, AR, AP (Inventory later)
Type of business:	High growth electronic manufacturing
Type of conversion:	From manual to micro

Susan Hart has kept the books for a number of companies for at least 10 years. She knows what needs to be done and when it needs to be done. She used a micro-accounting package at the last company she worked at, so she knew the advantages firsthand.

When she took over the accounting department of ABC Manufacturing in June 1983, she knew what she wanted to do. The management was projecting $2 million in revenues for 1983, $4 million in 1984, and $10 million in 1987. She could see that their current system was not going to be able to handle that growth satisfactorily and felt that a micro-accounting system would answer all of their accounting and management requirements. They had no unusual needs, no special ways of doing any of the accounting. Also, ABC already had several PCs used for nonaccounting purposes, so she knew that she could get some knowledgeable help from within the company.

So she went out shopping for a system. She knew that the accounting software she had used before was very limited in both capacity and flexibility, and she wanted something better. She decided to get separate general ledger, accounts receivable, and accounts payable modules that would work as an integrated system. She planned to approach computerizing their inventory later, after the accounting was up and running smoothly. She also knew that she only needed a single-user system. She spent several weeks visiting computer stores. There were a number of computer stores close to ABC, and she felt it would be advantageous to buy from one of them so that support would be close at hand.

She asked each computer store she visited to show her a flexible system on a single-user micro. Several of the stores would not demonstrate accounting systems. They told her that there were too many variables for them to say for sure that a certain package would fit her needs. They said she could study the manuals in the store and make her own decision. Other stores claimed their packages would handle her needs and offered a demonstration using some sample data that they had set up for such purposes.

One store impressed her with their forthrightness and the overall structure of the deal. They told her that their high-end accounting package was fairly new for micros, but it had been running on minicomputers before being translated. They said they had compared several different packages and selected this one as the most flexible, easiest to use, and having the best accounting controls. They said this package was one that supported its end-users with a toll-free telephone number, but they recommended that she hire a consultant to help with the software selection and setup.

Susan called the software company and asked about the software and the support. They said that their software did not require the use of a consultant; the software would handle her needs; and they had had many customers successfully set up just by using their telephone support. She decided to buy that system, which was a dual diskette PC, and three modules of the accounting software. The total price came to $6,000; $3,600 for the PC and $2,400 for the accounting software. (ABC already had a printer.)

The PC was delivered in July, and the software arrived in August. Susan began the conversion. She was disappointed that the flexible report formatter required her to design her statements from scratch. None were supplied with the system. It took her an extra week to learn how to format the reports and set up the required formats. Later, when she had the general ledger up and running, she found that if she added a new account to the chart of accounts, the formats had to be changed. The program didn't allow such editing. Susan had to go back and set up the new formats from scratch.

She then moved on to the accounts payable module. This was installed without undue struggle until it was time to integrate it with the general ledger module. Her attempts to do so failed. In fact, whenever she instructed the accounts payable module to post to the general ledger, numerous changes occurred throughout her ledger at random. The software vendor acknowledged that there was a bug (error) in the program that caused this to happen, but they would not be correcting it for five or six months. (Note that if Susan had not known to back up her data files prior to attempting the module integration, she would have had to go through the setup all over again for the general ledger.)

Then Susan went to the accounts receivable module. It was soon clear that the module did not produce invoices, and that was one feature she required. The software company informed her that their program handled invoicing, but not in the accounts receivable module; if she required invoices, she would have to purchase both inventory and order entry modules. At the store she was told that if she needed to run all five of those modules, she would also need to buy a hard disk for her system. Since she had already put in so much effort into the project, she decided to make the additional purchases. These came to $1,200 for the two modules and $2,200 for the hard disk: a new total of $9,400.

Susan continued with the installation. She soon came to a major hurdle. It seemed that the invoicing feature insisted on relieving inventory and would only work if inventory were also set up. The software company confirmed this feature and was not planning to change it. It also became clear that the system could not handle returns of merchandise by customers. Susan was understandably annoyed, and her relationship with the software company soon became a confrontation. After accusations on both sides (the software company claimed that none of their thousands of other users had had any such problems), Susan managed to arrange a return of the software.

Susan had now been working on the conversion for over five months and decided to hire a consultant to help out. She made a list of her requirements this time; it was six pages long. The consultant felt Susan's needs were not unusual and was familiar with a program that could handle most of the items on her list. Some of the items were not available in any software package but could be accomplished by using some special accounting techniques to get around the limitations of the programs.

Susan had the same store order the new software. It cost about $1,500 less than the first brand, partly because only three modules were needed. However, the 4,000 three-part checks that had been printed up to work with the first brand of software could not be used with the new brand. Also, Susan decided she would not return the hard disk, even if she could, because she appreciated its performance advantages and anticipated needing it later.

At this point, Susan was in a hurry. The books were in fairly good shape, but they were several months behind because of the ongoing conversion attempt. ABC had not seen a financial statement in over three months. Nevertheless, the consultant advised that they start with a single module. Susan picked accounts receivable as the most important.

Susan's experience meant that she did not need as much of the consultant's help as a beginner might. She mainly needed training in the "secrets" of the new accounting software and in how to accomplish certain things that were not specifically built into the software. The conversion of all three modules was accomplished fairly smoothly over the next two months. Susan paid the consultant $1,500, and considered herself lucky to have achieved a successful conversion.

ABC Building Management

Who did it:	Owner
Accounting needs:	Complex—GL, AR, AP
Type of business:	Commercial property management
Type of conversion:	From outside service to micro

John Fletcher owns and manages two large commercial office buildings. He has about 300 tenants leasing office space in the two buildings. To these tenants he also offers such services as an answering service, mailbox rentals, photocopying, and warehouse storage facilities. This results in about 700 charges to the 300 accounts each month.

Before computerizing, John had a computer service bureau do his monthly billings and used an outside CPA to do the rest of the accounting and prepare financial statements on a monthly basis. His monthly fees for these services were running around $200 for the service bureau and $300 for the CPA. He generally received the financial statements four to six weeks after the end of the month. His office staff consisted of an office manager and a secretary. Neither John nor his staff had any previous experience with computers other than preparing the billing information each month for the service bureau.

John's primary reasons for wanting to computerize his accounting records were to cut the costs of the outside accounting services and to get his accounting information faster. He felt that his current office staff would be sufficient to operate the computerized system

He started shopping for a computer in December 1982. After visiting stores and dealers for about a month, John knew he needed help, but he didn't know where to turn. In January he attended a workshop about microcomputing offered by the local Chamber of Commerce. One of the speakers was a CPA, so he contacted her and engaged her firm to assist him with the selection of the computer system and to help get it up and running.

John felt he needed one of the specialized property management software packages. It was important for his system to monitor individual leases: their individual costs and income per square foot, their expiration dates, and the amounts of extra services he supplied. He also required repetitive monthly billings and was concerned that the various accounting functions be done correctly.

John and the CPA firm spent the next three months researching property management packages, both together and independently. After they had looked at about 10 packages without finding anything adequate, John became frustrated and considered keeping things the way they were. The CPA proposed that he consider adapting a flexible, general-purpose accounting system for his accounting and use a spreadsheet to track the leases and special services. She showed John how it could work, and he agreed with the concept.

But he wanted to try one other route first. He contacted the Institute of Real Estate Management and asked what they knew about property management software. Their reply was that they had researched it fairly extensively and had not found any programs that met their standards. They recommended the same approach that the CPA had suggested.

It was now April. John and the CPA settled on a general-purpose accounting package and a popular spreadsheet program for the spreadsheet applications. John had seen a lot of hardware over the previous four months. The IBM XT had just been released in late March, and he decided to get one. For a printer he selected a Toshiba 1350 that could produce both high-speed dot matrix print and a very presentable near-letter-quality print at a lower speed. His system costs were about $6,000 for the XT, $2,300 for the printer, and $3000 for the software.

John's XT did not arrive until June. He then ordered the software and received it in about a week. The Toshiba was delayed, and John was provided with an Epson printer as a loaner until his arrived. The conversion of the accounts receivable began in early July. A college student was hired to enter the information on the 300 tenant accounts, their balance forward amounts, and the monthly recurring journal entries. This data entry took about four weeks to complete, including checking and verification.

The office manager was trained by the CPA firm to do the accounting for the accounts receivable program. She had no previous accounting experience. About four hours of training were enough to get her up and running, even though she did not understand everything she was doing. Step-by-step documentation was also provided, similar to the sample in Appendix F. The CPA was not needed for further training, although she did spend time overseeing and checking the parallel runs. The accounts receivable was going well enough by August that they started the general ledger conversion.

John's general ledger and financial statements were complex. He had five departments: building 1, building 2, answering service, photocopying, and G&A (general & administrative). Initially, he wanted to make some fairly extensive changes to his chart of accounts. After discussion with the CPA, he agreed to wait until December, the end of his fiscal year. She felt that the changes would make the conversion more difficult, especially with such an inexperienced staff.

The conversion of the general ledger took four days of the CPA's time, followed by about four hours of training for the office manager. Additional support by the CPA firm was much heavier for the general ledger and consisted mostly of accounting questions rather than computer questions.

Two occurrences interfered with these conversions. In late August a complete remodeling was begun on the firm's offices. Also, John had redesigned the tenant statements for the computer system, and there was a two-month delay in their delivery. The remodeling required that the computer be removed and stored in an office down the hall to protect it from dust and debris. Because of these problems, those two conversions were not actually completed until October, a total of about four months. By the time the computer was caught up with the old system, the office manager had done four parallel runs and was comfortable with the new system.

The next step was the accounts payable module. The new checks had already arrived, and the conversion was relatively simple. It was completed within about two weeks, but integration to the general ledger was put off until John's staff had worked with it for about two months.

John's changeover took about 10 months from initial decision to completion, including all of the unexpected delays. His tangible costs were about $12,000 for hardware and software and about $5,000 for the consultant's help with the conversion and training.

ABC Financial Planning and Management Company

Who did it:	General Manager
Accounting needs:	Typical—GL, AR, AP—cash basis
Type of business:	Financial services
Type of conversion:	From in-house minicomputer to micro

ABC is a small service corporation with 20 employees. It has about 700 clients, but only about 30 percent are active at any one time. Prior to the conversion of the accounting system, the accounting for the general ledger and accounts payable was being done on the firm's IBM SYSTEM/34 minicomputer. The accounts receivable were being done manually. There were four or five people involved with the accounting, each doing a small part of it. No one was strong in accounting, and there was often some confusion and wasted effort involved in the accounting process. The monthly reports were generally weeks late. ABC used a CPA firm to generate their annual financial statements.

Jim Williams had been the general manager of ABC for about 2 years. He was paying $6,000 per year for the license to his accounting software, just for the general ledger and accounts payable functions. It would cost him an additional $6,000 per year to add accounts receivable functions. His four-person data-processing staff (and the minicomputer) were already spending much of their time on accounting tasks when there were many more profitable things they could be working on. In addition to the minicomputer, the firm had three or four Xerox microcomputers, which were used for word processing and database applications (not for accounting).

Jim felt that they might be able to move their accounting system to a microcomputer if he also hired an accountant to operate the system. He talked to several computer consultants and CPA firms and found that it was both possible and relatively inexpensive to convert ABC's accounting to a smaller computer. He also found out that the selection of the accounting software would require a lot of research by someone familiar with ABC's particular needs.

In August Jim saw an announcement of a presentation to be given by a CPA about selecting microcomputer accounting systems. He contacted that CPA firm and asked what they could do for him. They did not see any problem with fitting his volumes of accounts and transactions onto a micro. They said they would come to his office to analyze his current system, and discuss improvements possible by using a microcomputer system. He hired them to do that, and then they discussed several systems that would fit his needs in varying degrees. They told him the trade-offs of each system: some cost more, some required more manual operations, some had inadequate instruction manuals; none were just what he needed.

The CPA firm described to him what would be involved in the conversion and recommended that ABC hire an accountant to operate the system. Jim had already decided that he wanted to get an IBM XT computer, unless the CPA firm found a reason to choose something different. He wanted a fast printer that would only be used for accounting, so he didn't need a letter-quality printer. An Okidata ML84 was recommended.

Jim liked the step-by-step approach that the CPAs described to him and told them he would like to start right away. Although he would be hiring an accountant to learn and operate the new system, it was agreed that his Data Processing Department should do the data entry parts of the conversion. He bought the recommended system in late September, hired a June accounting graduate, and they set to work.

The general ledger was to be done first, since the financial statements were the worst problem area of the current system. It took about two weeks to get the general ledger up and running, although there was additional time used for verifying its operation (the parallel runs, as discussed in Chapter 4). One part of the conversion was to restructure the chart of accounts. One digit needed to be trimmed off of each account number so that it would fit the constraints of the program. This was easy in this case, since almost all of the old account numbers had ended in zeros. Several new accounts were added, also.

At the end of the fiscal year, November 30th, the

closing of the books was delayed several months while ABC waited for some critical information from their accountants (whose offices had recently burnt down). The microcomputer accounting system could go ahead with the new year's accounting even though the previous year had not yet been closed. The minicomputer system could not. When the figures arrived from the accountants, the previous year was closed in just one-half hour on the micro. After six days of unsuccessfully trying to get the numbers to balance correctly on the minicomputer, ABC gave up. They never did get the year closed on the minicomputer; they just decided to shut down that accounting system, since the micro system was working so well.

Meanwhile, ABC began the accounts receivable conversion in November. The experienced data-entry staff took only 5 hours to input the initial information on all 700 clients. The accounts receivable conversion could have taken just 2 or 3 weeks, but there were several other projects that interrupted the conversion. As a result, this conversion was spread over two and a half months.

Typical of accounting software at that time, ABC's new accounts receivable module would not support cash basis accounting if it were integrated to the general ledger module. As a result, ABC has to run the accounts receivable module on a stand alone basis, which means that ABC has to double-enter its cash receipts: once into the accounts receivable module and once into the general ledger module.

The accounts payable conversion began in January. The volume in this area was about 125 checks per month—not a large number for a computerized system. Unlike the accounts receivable module, the accounts payable module for this system does support cash basis accounting when it is integrated to the general ledger. This conversion was relatively fast and easy, helped by ABC's recent experience converting the general ledger and the accounts receivable modules. It was completed in about three weeks.

This was a typical micro-accounting conversion project in size, duration, and cost. The hardware cost about \$7,500, the software about \$2,200, and the consulting fees about \$5,000. ABC now receives its financial reports extremely quickly and is saving the $12,000 per year that the same accounting functions would cost on the IBM SYSTEM/34. As an added benefit, ABC's accounting system was improved in several areas during the conversion. The accounting system is now in good shape and can handle a lot of growth with little additional expense.

3

THE SELECTION PROCESS

3.1 THE MICRO MARKETPLACE

If you were going to spend several thousand dollars on any type of new equipment (such as a new copier or a new telephone system), you would watch out for several things. You would want to select the correct size for your needs and your budget. You would look into the reputation of the manufacturer and the seller, perhaps by talking with previous customers to see if they remained pleased after the sale. You would find out what support would be available and its cost. You might even have to consider the tradeoff between a tried and tested older model and an exciting new model.

These considerations are just as important in the selection of a microcomputer system, but there are some additional ones. The first is the fast-changing nature of these systems. Because of the continuing technological advances in microelectronics, the products have short shelf lives. New products are continually being announced, and most of them are great improvements over those of a year earlier. Unfortunately, it has become common for these announcements to precede availability by many months, and even that promised date often slips several times as the production department wrestles with reality. Thus the initial deliveries of a new product are best avoided; a seasoned shopper in the micro market waits a while longer, until the first users report their reactions.

A related problem is the shortage of information available on these products. There are so many products, and so many others that have come and gone, that any one dealer cannot know them all. Each product, whether hardware or software, is extremely complex. It takes months of continued use to completely learn any of these products.

Hardware

The hardware area of today's microcomputer market is no longer as volatile and confusing as a few years ago. while there are still a large number of microcomputer manufacturers out there, their products are well designed and proven through use. There is no longer much risk that the hardware might not work reliably. The systems even look alike. It has become difficult to tell one "portable" micro from another, or one PC from another, without reading the label.

As a result of this standardization, the selection of your business computer no longer has to include a computer hardware design analysis. The biggest risk you have today is to buy some hardware that runs fine and then not be able to find a software package that fits your needs. Even worse, that software may be readily available, but not for your particular PC. This is one reason the IBM PC has been so popular, despite its well-known drawbacks (the keyboard layout and the overpricing). There are systems on the market that run several times as fast for the same price. But the IBM PC and XT guarantee the most compatibility with new developments, and in this fast-moving field that is an important consideration.

Software

Microcomputer software products are not as mature as the hardware. The software application packages that you buy to run on your system adhere to no particular set of standards; in fact, most of them explicitly disclaim all warranties of quality and performance. The quality of the accounting programs varies greatly, and not always with any relation to the price, the slick packaging, or the name of a major company on the cover. There are some powerful and flexible packages available, but even the software houses and retail dealers don't know which is best. New packages and upgrades to old packages appear frequently, and their complexity discourages ongoing evaluation efforts.

Each increase in the speed or capacity of the hardware makes it easier to write programs. What this means is that a new program can be far better than an older one, but this only happens if the newer program is based on the best of the old and has built onto that base.

Many of the microcomputer accounting programs were originally written to fit the needs of one specific business situation (and it is sometimes evident that accounting professionals were not involved in the design). Even with enhancements added over the years, this type of program is not very flexible. The concept of a general-purpose accounting program being offered to the mass market is still new, and the current ones all have limitations.

We were once so naive to believe that any accounting program offered on the market would at least accomplish the basic accounting functions, however inelegantly. That was when we also learned that most vendors consider such software a nonreturnable item because of the possibility of your copying the diskettes and the manuals.

The ease with which software can be copied is one reason the prices of software are so high. The software developers put in thousands of hours to develop the packaged product and need to sell many systems before they start making any money on that product. The microcomputer software industry estimates that for every copy of a program sold, about eight to 10 copies are pirated (not paid for).

For a business user, it is wiser to buy the software from an authorized dealer. The software companies keep track of the software packages' serial numbers and buyers. Only registered users are able to receive ongoing support from the software company and/or its dealers. This includes responding to problems, answering questions, and supplying upgrades to the software. Software is complex and fragile. Any accounting software you buy (actually, you just license it) is the beginning of an ongoing relationship with the company that developed that package.

Given this state of the micro marketplace, what is the best way to approach it, make your selection, and purchase a system that will meet your needs over the next few years? The rest of Chapter 3 tells how to go about it.

3.2 YOUR ALTERNATIVES

Hiring a Consultant

If you have decided that your business is ready for a microcomputer accounting system, then you are ready for the next major step: choosing which one. The ideal person to carry out this selection process is one who knows accounting theory and practice, who knows all of the microcomputers available, who has set up and used all of the accounting software available, and who knows your business as well as you do.

More realistically, you are likely to be best served by an accounting firm or a computer consultant who specializes in accounting applications. But you must be cautious in choosing your help. The right choice can save you much frustration and many misspent hours and dollars. The wrong choice will not save you much of anything, although it will probably cost you about the same amount. The important criteria to look for are independence, expertise, experience, and compatibility.

You want *independent* consultants so you can be assured that their recommendations are objective, based on your needs rather than any compensation they might receive. There are numerous computer consultants in business, but many of them are also dealers. This has been a traditional way of selling computers and software, long before retail computer stores appeared. The problem is the confusion between the terms consultant and dealer. When these dealers start calling themselves consultants, the other consultants have to be called "independent consultants." Anyway, be sure to ask if they sell anything besides their expertise.

The *expertise* you will require is quite specialized, a combination of accounting and microcomputers. Unfortunately, both of these fields are subject to "expertitis," where people suddenly become self-designated experts. Doing bookkeeping in a company's accounting department does not make someone an expert in accounting, just as working on a computer assembly line does not make someone knowledgeable about computer systems. Check your consultant's credentials; licenses, degrees, or certificates indicate a professional commitment in addition to assuring a certain level of expertise. There is a growing trend for consulting firms to add CPAs to their staffs and for CPA firms to hire computer experts. Either of these can provide a good combination of backgrounds to help you.

You need *experienced* help because both the hardware and the software are learned through a trial-and-error process. The instruction manuals have to cover every contingency, and many key details lie buried among irrelevancies. If you hire an accountant who has not already been through the process many times, then you will not receive much help. You will both spend a lot of time looking through piles of owners' manuals and going through demonstrations. So ask for at least four references—previous clients that will tell you how well they were helped—and be sure to call them.

Finally, you want your help to be *compatible* with you

and your methods. You will have to work with the consultant through some tough areas and some sensitive areas. You will be discussing what you need and want, what you want to spend, and when you want it done. You will have to show your consultant all of the details of your current accounting system. You will be relying on the consultant's judgment throughout the conversion process. If the personalities, methods, or working habits aren't right, then keep looking.

Hiring a consultant does not mean that you can then go on vacation and have it all done when you return. You will still have to make the decisions, based on the consultant's recommendations and your own judgment. You are the one taking the risks, the one who knows and cares most about your business. Ask all of those questions that come to you. Find out why that particular product or method is being recommended.

Doing it Yourself

If you choose to make the system selection on your own, try to cover all of the areas in Sections 3.5 and 3.6. Study a few system guidebooks and microcomputer magazines (see Appendix B). Make sure you work with several stores or dealers before making any decision. Insist on demonstrations, using some of your own accounting data that you have brought with you. Ask for the names of previous customers using the same hardware and software recommended to you; if there are none, then you are about to become a pioneer (often pictured with arrows in several places). Finally, get all of those promises of capabilities and after-sale support in writing; if it's not in writing, you certainly shouldn't count on it.

Note that this process will probably take you several months for the study, research, shopping, and demonstrations. With a consultant, it can take just a few hours or days. Unless you have some unusual needs, the selection process is not difficult for those who already know the micro-accounting marketplace. It is difficult for a newcomer.

3.3 WHERE DO YOU GET ONE?

While your consultant will help you select which hardware system and software packages suit your needs, you will probably have to make the actual purchase yourself. Once you know what you want, it is like buying a new car; you can shop around for the best deal, or you can just pay the published price. Consider both the price and the after-sale support. By support, we mean more than just answering your questions whenever you call. We mean installation and software setup assistance based on experience with that particular system, thus averting much of the trial-and-error learning. Most computer dealers will supply some free training of a general nature (not in micro-accounting) and will provide repair services for equipment they have sold, at fairly standard rates. Dealers vary widely in what they charge for maintenance contracts.

Before microcomputers appeared, computers were generally sold by the manufacturer's direct sales force and by system houses. System houses are companies that specialize in starting with a set of computer hardware and building it up to a complete system, usually appropriate for a specific industry or function. When a sale is made through these channels, the seller sends a team of experts to install the system, make sure it is working properly, and train the company's data processing staff on the new equipment. This is all included in the purchase price!

But the price of micros is so low that such support cannot be provided free of charge. The industry is still experimenting with different ways of selling micros and packaged software, trying to find which work best for both the seller and the customer. There are no rules, so you will have to be on your guard.

The two most common distribution channels are retail computer stores and mail-order houses. Both of these channels sell micros as off-the-shelf commodity items for you to take away, plug in, and use. Mail-order houses offer low prices and no support. A retail store will typically carry four or five levels of systems. The low end might be an IBM PCjr or an Apple IIe. Next would be one of the all-in-one "portable" PCs and perhaps the Apple MacIntosh. The next level might be the DEC line of micros or the IBM PC and XT. Finally, the store might also carry a PC networking system or a multi-user computer such as an Altos 586; these require a much more sophisticated user and should not be sold as off-the-shelf commodities. Increasingly, retail stores are working with one or more local accounting firms to help their business customers with both the selection and the conversion processes.

There are a few computer stores scattered around that have existed since the early days of micro retailing. They tend to have more expertise and handle more complex systems. Some of these also tend to recommend and sell older, proven systems that will get the job done, rather than the systems that are currently in the headlines.

There is another distribution channel, less well known because it is not operated from a retail storefront. Most of these dealers started as computer consultants, then decided they would no longer send their clients down to the local computer store. Since they were providing most of the support anyway, why should the store rake in all of those easy dollars? Some of these dealers sell the equipment and software at reduced prices; some don't. They also tend to carry the larger, multi-user computer systems, along with a staff of computer engineers and programmers necessary to support such installations. If there is a CPA on staff, these dealers offer a good channel for computerized accounting systems. Their prices may reflect an expected level of support. If you are already using a consultant, try not to pay twice for the same support.

Accounting firms are just starting to enter the microcomputer field. Much research and practice is required to gain expertise, but their clients are beginning to demand their help, and they are being drawn into it. Some of the accounting firms that enter the field soon decide to become dealers, perhaps following a line of reasoning similar to that of the consultants.

Notice how similar these last two dealer channels are to the traditional system house. The main difference is that micro systems are much smaller and cheaper than the large systems provided by system houses, so the support provided is not free. The order in which the prices and level of support increase through these various distribution channels is as follows: mail-order house, department store, computer store, and consultant-dealer.

All of these channels are also used by the computer "gray market." This is where the product being sold is not a standard product authorized by the manufacturer. The most widespread practice is to buy a "bare-bones" model of a computer, buy additional components at wholesale prices, and build up a more expensive model. There are many problems in this approach. The components used are not always identical to those the system was designed for. Because this is usually done to save money, the parts used may give inferior performance. They may even be used parts rather than new ones. Also, repair facilities usually insist that all of the components of a system be standard before they will work on it.

To avoid buying such a system, make sure that your supplier is an authorized dealer for that brand of equipment. You can also ask to talk to previous customers to see how happy they are with their systems.

So which channel is best for you? It depends on whether you will have a consultant helping you set up your system and on how you want to handle breakdowns and repairs. Without a consultant you should look for much more in the way of support. It is better to buy all of the pieces of your system from the same seller. If the various pieces don't work together, it will be clear who is responsible for helping you. Only if your consultant recommends some specific software packages and knows they will work with the intended hardware should you deviate from that policy and order the software from a mail-order house. (Mail-order savings are substantial: 25 to 40 percent off the list price.)

3.4 MAINTENANCE AND REPAIRS

Sooner or later your computer system will break down. With proper treatment and handling, it will continue working for you for five to ten years, but chances are great that it will require some repairs every year or two. One of the *diskette drives* may require realignment, or a cable may fray and break. The display screen may acquire a permanent image by being left on over a weekend with the brightness control turned up, or the printer can get so much use that its motor burns out. There are many minor problems that could seriously affect your business as you become more and more dependent on the computer.

Your best protection is a maintenance contract on your system. This is like health insurance for your computer, except the repairs are guaranteed regardless of the extent of the disorder. You can choose between carry-in, pick-up and delivery, and on-site coverage, and between various response times, depending on your needs and your budget. These contracts are sometimes offered by computer stores (usually just for the equipment purchased there). For the IBM PC, XT, and PCjr, they are offered through repair centers nationwide by MAI/Sorbus, by IBM Corporation, by Xerox Corporation, and by various local companies. Digital Equipment Corporation and Hewlett-Packard have established repair facilities in major cities, where users can take those brands of PCs to be repaired.

What if you don't have a maintenance contract and your system goes down? Most of the repair facilities already listed will accept certain equipment without a contract on a carry-in basis. The repairs are done on an hourly rate plus parts, at a lower priority than the contract repairs. The store where you purchased the equipment should handle it similarly. Some items, such as hard disk drives, have to be sent back to the factory for any repairs. Because this may take many weeks, a good service center will be able to arrange a loaner to keep your system running for that period—but they don't have to. With a contract they do have to, sometimes free of charge.

One last consideration is that if you add to your system and have two or more of any system component, then you have additional options whenever something fails. For example, if you have several printers and one breaks down, your operations may be able to continue by sharing the remaining printers. This means that breakdowns may not be so critical, and you can go for a cheaper maintenance contract.

3.5 IS A REQUEST FOR PROPOSAL NECESSARY? A CONTRACT?

The Request For Proposal (RFP) and the Request for Price Quotation (RPQ) are traditional ways of shopping for computer systems. They are essentially bidding processes. The buyer sends out copies of a detailed requirements list to the various vendors and waits for them all to respond with descriptions and prices of their solutions. For this process to be effective, every detail must be listed and responded to.

For microcomputers, the process cannot be so formal. The stores and dealers cannot afford to spend the time to compile and send answers to such detailed requests unless they are fairly confident increased sales will result. The prices and the merchandise just do not vary that much among retail vendors. Most computer stores are run more along the lines of automobile dealerships than traditional computer system houses; thus it is more appropriate for them to sell on the basis of their images and the support they offer.

If you have a special need that the standard software packages cannot handle, put it in writing and send it to a list of vendors. Some will respond, especially the dealers with more expertise. You would probably need some degree of custom programming, and that means hiring an expensive programmer by the hour. The bidding process is a good way to see how much it might cost, and how long it might take. And this brings up the subject of customization.

Years ago, every new computer required some custom programming; it was just part of the usual installation and maintenance. Programs were written with the expectation that professional programmers would be involved with the setup and use of the program. But for PCs, customized business software is neither usual nor desirable. Although some of the older accounting software packages for PCs were designed to be altered by programmers, the newer packages have been designed with enough flexibility built in to handle most situations. For the basic accounting functions, it would take a large-scale effort (years of programming time) to design and build a program that is as good as the better packages now available.

A customized accounting system, whether by altering a standard accounting package or building a complete accounting system, should be avoided if it all possible. The costs are usually high, and the project can drag on and on. Problems usually arise because the results desired were not originally specified in sufficient detail and seem to change as time goes by. The programmer may request changes, or you may come up with some additional ideas.

When the project does end and you think the program is working adequately, you must still consider the maintenance of the program. Packaged software is supported by its publisher and its dealers (in varying degrees)—answering your questions, fixing problems when they appear, and offering upgrades and improvements. If you just made a large investment in the development of a custom program, you will need someone to support your use of it over the years. Packaged software does not have a good reputation for support, but custom software has a much worse reputation. Most programmers dislike working on some other programmer's past efforts. Anyway, you get the picture: more problems.

If you need custom programming, use a contract. This will allow you to specify the details, and it will require the programmers to adhere to a schedule. The payments should be spread out along the term of the project, conditional on the demonstrated and tested completion of each phase. The negotiations and the contract should include who will retain the ownership rights to the program. Any programmer writing microcomputer programs for businesses should be accustomed to such contracts. Have your attorney check such a contract before it is signed.

3.6 WHAT TO LOOK FOR (AND LOOK OUT FOR) IN ACCOUNTING SOFTWARE

When shopping for accounting software, there are five areas to focus on: the general ledger, the support, the ease of use, the reports, and the security (see Figure 3.1). We will

The
Five Major Considerations
When Shopping for Accounting Software

- GENERAL LEDGER
  - Flexible Chart of Accounts
  - Flexible Report Formats for Financial Statements

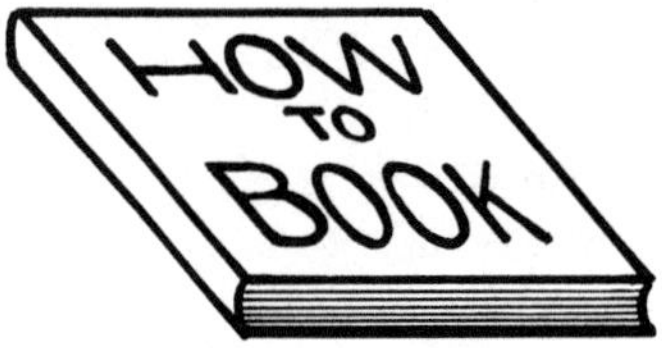

- DOCUMENTATION
  - Easy-to-follow Instructions
  - Tutorial
  - Sample Reports

- EASE OF USE
  - System Setup
  - Daily Operations Flow Smoothly

- REPORTS
  - Clear, Easy to Read

- SECURITY
  - Good Audit Trails
  - Passwords

FIGURE 3.1

discuss each area in depth and then give a brief summary of all five.

General Ledger

Even if you are planning to convert some other facet of your accounting, such as accounts receivable, look first at the general ledger modules of those brands you are considering. You will surely want to convert your general ledger at some point, for its reports will provide you with information on your financial situation, both the overview and the detail. You will want to use the same brand of software as your other accounting applications so they will operate together automatically. You will also minimize the amount of learning involved. The different modules of a single brand of software are generally designed with similar screens and operations, making it easy to shift between the various modules.

The general ledger is the basis on which the whole accounting system is established. All of your financial transactions will end up in the general ledger (hopefully), and your financial statements will be prepared from it. To make the transition easier and the results acceptable, you want to be sure that your computerized general ledger is consistent with your current accounting practices.

The best way to be assured of a good match is to find a general ledger package with sufficient flexibility. Such a general ledger will accept your chart of accounts as it is. A less flexible package may have already set up certain parameters for numbering or ordering accounts that cannot be changed. If your present numbering system doesn't fit into those parameters, you will have to change it. That means a lot of extra work and retraining.

The other important benefit of a flexible system is that you can design your financial statements. You don't have to accept a format you don't like or one that doesn't fit your needs. For example, service businesses have different needs than manufacturers do. When the software is designed to always show a cost of goods sold section on the income statement, that report looks a little strange for most service businesses (they usually have no inventories).

Some other important features you might desire in your general ledger are budgets, departments, recurring monthly journal entries, reversing entries, and bank *reconciliations.* The budgets are sometimes just one figure for the whole year, allocated one-twelfth per month; other packages allow you to enter a different figure for each month and let you choose between monthly or year-to-date budgetary reports. The departments should generate their own statements, as well as a combined statement and a combined statement with detail by department. The recurring monthly entries can be quite important in some business situations. Bank reconciliations are very handy and simple to implement, yet few general ledgers include that feature.

Support

The ideal support system for an off-the-shelf accounting software package would include evaluation aids, instruction and training aids, an installation manual, a system manager's manual, a setup manual, an operations manual, a dealer knowledgeable about the features and installation procedures, and a network of accounting firms knowledgeable about the setup and use of the system. You won't find much of this yet, but they are moving in the right direction and should get there in a year or two.

The support that comes with a typical package right now is a thick owner's manual for each module. This manual may have information about all the right subjects, but you never seem to be able to answer the question at hand. Here's a common example: Your computer tells you there has been an Error #123. You look that up in the manual and find, "Error 123: system attempted to access beyond end of file." The problem may turn out to be that you have not yet completed the proper setup operation on your new data diskette, but you won't find a hint of that in the manual.

A similar problem occurs when the manual tells you how to do an operation, step by step, but offers no help for when you make that inevitable error. You have stepped off the lighted path, into the vast darkness that seems to have no escape. Everyone reacts to this situation the same way: with panic. And with good reason—you have been left no recourse but trial and error, and each try seems more likely to result in disaster than success. Several programs recognize this problem and offer a simple solution, such as pushing the ESCAPE key to retreat to the beginning of the path from any situation.

Computer and programming jargon remains a problem throughout some manuals. You may think you know what a record sounds like and what a field looks like, but don't make any bets. Anyway, look for a manual that talks to you in English, unless you have a data processing department to give it to. Also check out the index (if there is one). A good one is a necessity!

The organization of the manual and the readability of the individual pages are important. You will not read it as a novel. You will be constantly leafing through it looking for one tiny piece of information. But only at first: After you have decoded and memorized the 25 percent that is relevant to your situation, the manual will spend most of its time sitting on your shelf collecting dust.

Look at the tutorials offered for the system. A tutorial is a set of step-by-step lessons that walk a new user through the program. A good one takes you through setting up new accounts, recording several types of transactions, posting those transactions, making backup copies of the data, printing reports, and closing the accounting period. It also helps immensely if there is a tutorial to take you through the setup of a mini-company, going through the same steps that you will have to take to set up your company. Such a practice run is a necessity, because few people are able to correctly set up their computerized accounting system on the first try. It is easiest to practice if the answers are in the manual, so you can check your progress as you go along and know that you are correct.

Sometimes tutorials come on diskettes. When inserted into the computer, the tutorial diskette will lead you through the lessons interactively. It will tell you what to do next and watch to see how you do it. It will tell you immediately when you make a mistake and tell you the correct operation.

The worst tutorials are those interspersed throughout

the manual, usually following the reference section on each subject. The idea must be that you read one reference section, then do the tutorial on that subject, then move on to the next subject, and so on. That is not how people learn to use computer programs. Most want to sit down and go through the whole tutorial at once. While it is best to read the manual before going through the tutorials, many people don't do that. Not only are interspersed tutorials hard to follow, but they get in the way later when you try to use the manual as a reference.

Also watch out for those tutorials that tell you to enter two transactions and print out six reports based on the sample data they have provided. Some even leave it up to you what to enter for the two transactions. It sure is easy, but unfortunately you don't learn anything.

Some of the newest packages offer what is called on-line help. This means that when a question comes up while you are using the program, you need only push the HELP key, and the computer display changes to a reference manual, already turned to the appropriate page for the operation you are using. The new Solomon III accounting package offers this, and it seems to have the entire manual in there.

Also check to see if the software house offers a telephone number for you to call when your dealer can't answer your question. Some offer a toll-free number, some require an annual fee to take your calls, and some flatly refuse to talk to you.

Ease of Use

Ease of use means that the system helps rather than hinders the various operations. This includes the setup of the system as well as the daily operations.

The ease of the system setup is important, even though it is only done once (you hope). The setup is never simple, but if it is too difficult, the users have to resort to trial-and-error tactics. This becomes very frustrating and can result in an incorrect or less-than-optimal system. It can also result in the whole project being shelved, put off indefinitely out of frustration.

The first step of the setup is getting the programs properly loaded onto diskettes or hard disk, ready for use. The programs come on diskettes, but those are never the ones you work with. These originals become some of the backup copies you store and protect. Every brand of computer has different requirements for loading the programs, yet some software publishers insist on covering all of the different brands and equipment configurations in one manual. For the computer beginner, loading the programs is hard enough without having to sift through a lot of meaningless computer commands to find the ones that apply.

When you are out shopping for the software, read the section of the manual about loading the programs, and see if you can follow the steps for the equipment you are considering. We have seen manuals that told us to use a PIP command or an OPEN-APPLE key, when the computer involved didn't have either of those items. The software company managed to convert the programs to run on a new computer, but it forgot to convert the manuals.

Once the program is up and running on your computer, you are ready to set up your accounting system. Some programs give little information on how to approach it, what order to go through the steps, and especially what to do if everything doesn't go perfectly. Do you have to start over from scratch, or can you change anything at any time? Do they provide a walk-through (tutorial) for you to practice on, to help you get past the trial-and-error stages?

After considering the setup, you should look at the overall system design. Look for underlying metaphors, in which the computer operations relate to items and operations familiar from your manual system. This makes the system easier to visualize: how the data flows through, where it is stored, how it is combined, and how it can be extracted into useful information. Look at how the data input display screens are laid out, the order in which the information is requested, and the terminology used; does it look and sound familiar? If it is easier for you to visualize, it will be easier for you and your staff to learn it and use it.

Related to the overall design is the system's flow. This is a combination of communication ability and speed. A display screen can contain too much information or too little; the result will be slower operation and/or increased errors. Too many blanks to fill in or options to choose from will require time to stop and search through the screen, which will slow down editing operations. The other extreme is a string of questions, each thrown up on the screen by itself. You have to answer each one, then wait for the next screen to appear, never knowing exactly when the questions will end and the operation begin. You should be able to look at the screen and have a good idea what is going to happen next for each option you might choose. Cryptic abbreviations and programming jargon are unnecessary hindrances.

A display that lists several options and then waits for you to select one of those options, is called a *menu* display (see Figure 3.2). They are highly desirable while learning the program, but they slow down proficient users of the program. At that point the user no longer needs to study the alternatives and make a decision. Advanced programs recognize this and, by timing the response times, will only offer a menu when there is hesitation in the responses. Most accounting programs always produce their menus or else have no menus.

The speed factor comes in mainly as delays between screen changes and during sorting and posting operations. Delays of over 8 to 10 seconds are too long; by then your thoughts have begun to wander and you have to spend time collecting them when the next screen appears. Operations are also much more efficient if the program warns you that the current operation is going to take a while and rings a bell when it is finished. The computer could even estimate fairly closely how long it will take and tell you. For the longer operations, which can take several hours for a large amount of data, a graphic display of the time remaining would help your scheduling and assure you that the processing is indeed proceeding.

There are various other helpful features to look for. The backup operations are extremely important. They will have to be done after each data entry session and at the end of each month (see Section 5.4). Yet many accounting programs send you to the computer's operating system to

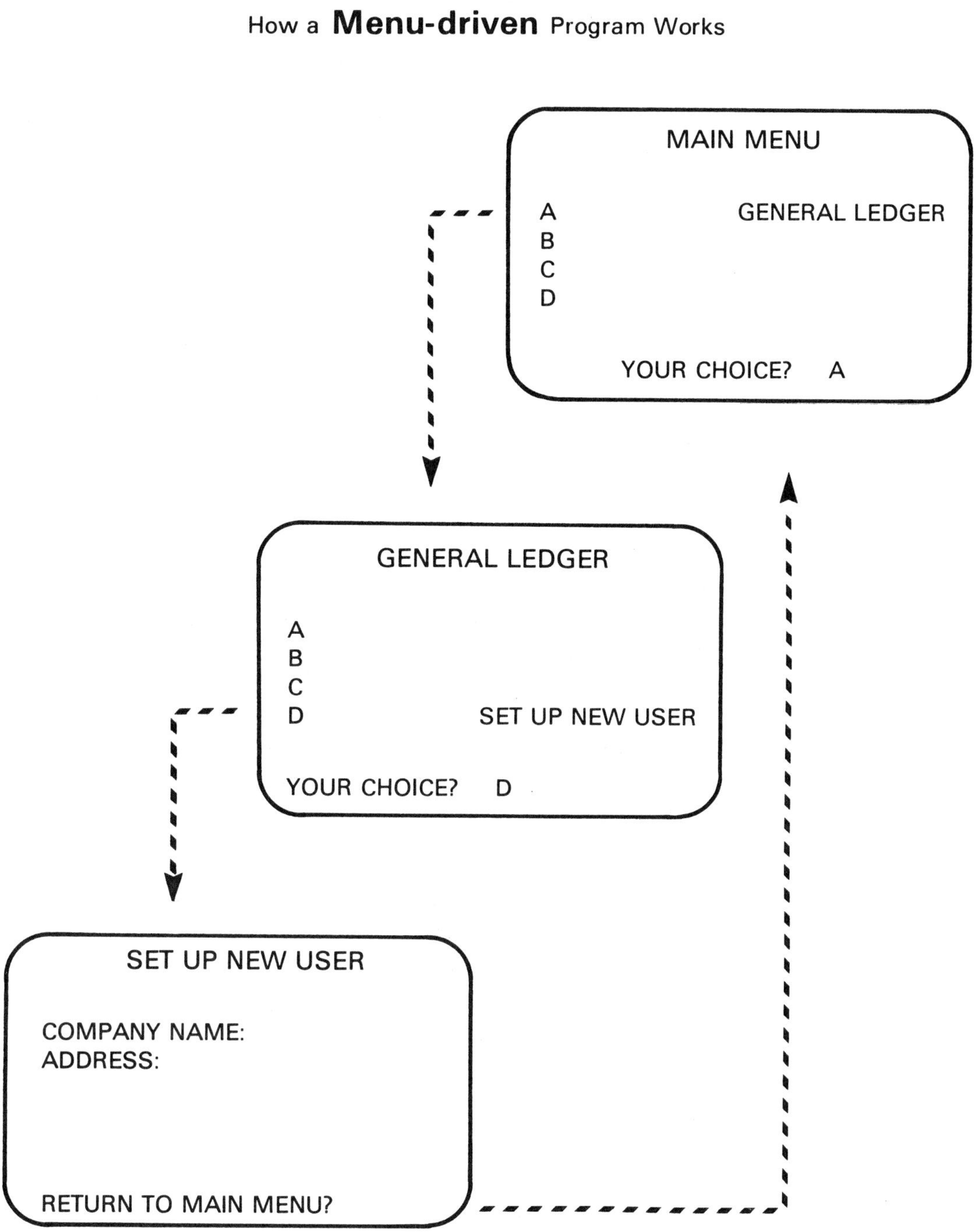
How a Menu-driven Program Works
MAIN MENU
A GENERAL LEDGER
B
C
D
YOUR CHOICE? A
GENERAL LEDGER
A
B
C
D SET UP NEW USER
YOUR CHOICE? D
SET UP NEW USER
COMPANY NAME:
ADDRESS:
RETURN TO MAIN MENU?

FIGURE 3.2

accomplish this, a difficult method that you just shouldn't have to go through. The commands involved look like so much gibberish, and yet if you leave out one of the characters or spaces, strange and/or disastrous things can happen to your data. There is no reason the programs can't build in backup operations appropriate for an accounting system; some brands already do so, to a limited extent.

For a floppy diskette system, it is valuable to know when you are running out of room on your data diskette and what to do about it. Most give you no information on either subject or refer you once more to your mysterious operating system. Newer programs now tell you how many transactions will fit in the remaining space or the percentage of space remaining.

Reports

Accounting systems vary greatly in the types of reports produced and in how you request them. Some systems force the printing of reports during data entry and posting operations, as audit trails for those operations. That really slows your operations down, so more efficient methods are preferable. Some other systems accumulate the audit trail information internally for later printing (and others don't provide audit trails at all—efficient but not recommended). Most systems allow you to call up information on one particular account to the display screen. A few systems allow you to send any report to either the display screen or to the printer, and perhaps even scroll the displayed report backwards and forwards (since you can only see part of the report at any time).

A report queue is very handy when you have a series of reports to be printed. It allows you to list the reports desired, after which it will print them all out for you. While you should monitor the printer for jamming or problems, you don't have to keep returning to the computer to request the next report (see Figure 3.3). Since you will probably want the same set of reports each week and month, it is also handy to be able to store such lists of reports for repeated use. This is a very nice feature.

FIGURE 3.3 The Advantage of a Print Queue

The reports produced by a computer generally come in two standard sizes, 8½ x 11 inches and 11 x 14 inches (see Figures 3.4 and 3.5). The smaller size is easier to work with and easier to store. There is a tendency with the larger size to try to squeeze too much detail onto it. When that happens, very few of the reports get read. It's just too much detail for anyone to absorb, and it makes it much harder to locate the information that you do want to see. Usually, the wider reports require a wider printer.

The type of printer used affects the quality of the reports. Printers commonly output four type styles, each of which affects the speed of the printing as well as the appearance of the report. The styles are dot matrix, compressed dot matrix, near-letter quality, and letter quality (see Figure 3.5). The first three styles use groupings of tiny dots to form the letters. The compressed style allows you to put on letter-size paper all of the information that normally fits on a 11" x 14" page. The near-letter quality uses extra dots to form the letters, so they will more closely resemble a typewriter's printing. The letter-quality print is the same as typewriter print, because it uses the same method; a hammer hits a letter down onto the paper, with an inked ribbon between.

Dot matrix printers, which produce the first three styles, are much cheaper and much faster than letter-quality printers. However, the compressed and near-letter-quality modes are much slower than the standard dot matrix. Different brands of printers require different commands from the software to put them into the various modes. Most accounting software is set only for letter quality or standard dot matrix. Some ask you for the code that will switch your printer into compressed mode and then let you print your wide reports compressed onto standard 8½" x 11" paper.

There are two types of reports generated by accounting systems: fixed format reports and flexible format reports. Fixed format reports cannot be changed, and every program has some. Look at the sample reports in the manuals. They should not be too cluttered nor have too many unintelligible abbreviations.

Types of Report Formats

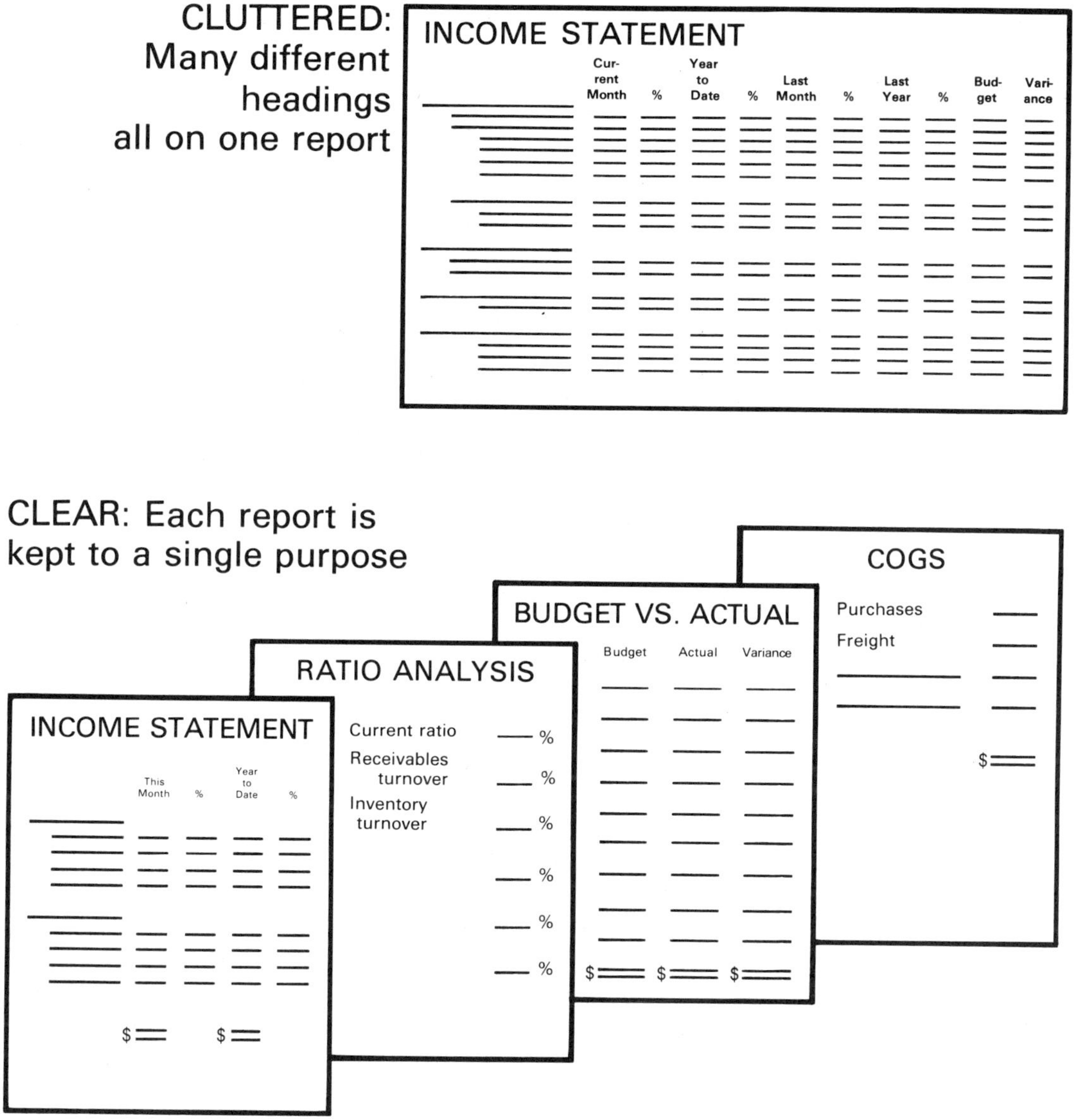

SUCH SUPPLEMENTARY SCHEDULES ARE AVAILABLE WITH SOME FLEXIBLE FORMAT PROGRAMS.

FIGURE 3.4

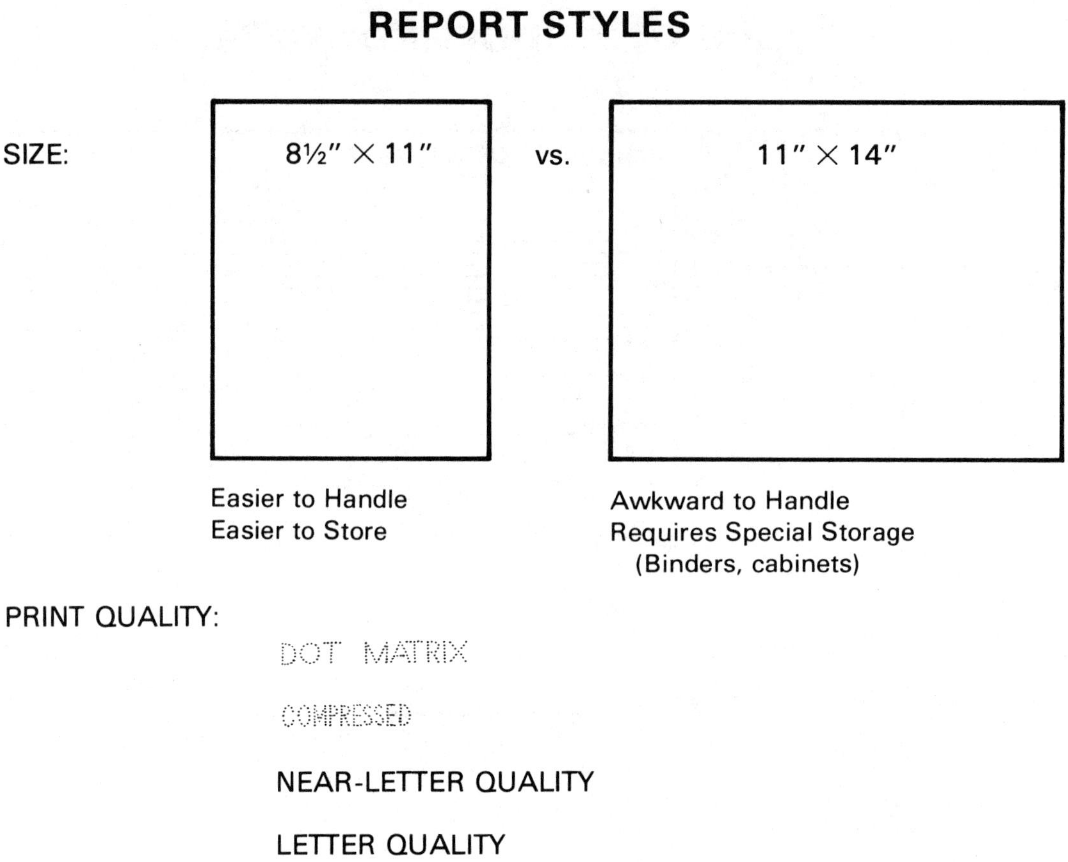

FIGURE 3.5 Report Styles and Print Quality

Some accounting programs come with all of the reports already designed, which may or may not fit your needs. Others allow you varying degrees of flexibility in designing your financial statements and additional management reports. It is common for the chart of accounts to be used to structure the balance sheet and the income statement. This is done by having you assign each account number to a category, such as title, subtotal 1, subtotal 2, posting account, and so on. This allows only one set of financial statement formats and is extremely difficult to set up (especially if you are not allowed to change account numbers or categories except by deleting the whole account). You cannot see how your design looks until everything is entered. It also means that the order of the accounts in your chart of accounts is the order in which they will appear on the reports. There are ways of formatting that are far easier to set up, try out, and change, and are far more flexible as well. These usually include a special program, a report generator, that you use only for formatting your reports.

Some of the programs come with very complex and sophisticated report generators or with ways of transferring the accounting data over to financial analysis programs (spreadsheets). They are not all easy to use, but they provide the means if you can provide or hire the expertise. They allow you to easily print out different sets of financial statements for different purposes and to avoid cramming too much data onto a report. You can use them to design reports for a single purpose (they are easier to follow) and use supplementary schedules to show additional detail, comparatives, budget variances, and so on. Check that such programs come with several examples that show both the formatting codes and the resulting report layout. They should also include a few formats already built. It may be easier for you to edit them than to start from scratch.

Security

As accountants, we find that being able to trust the system is our greatest concern, and it should be yours as well. Security in microcomputers is an area that has been largely ignored and avoided by the microcomputer industry, but if your business is large enough to be computerized, then it is large enough for you to worry about the security of the computer system. You need to consider three areas of security: system, data, and accounting.

System security means controlling the access to the accounting system. It concerns locked doors, keylock on/off switches, diskette library systems, and several levels of passwords. The first three items are rarely mentioned in your computer or accounting software manuals; the last is sometimes adequately provided, sometimes ignored.

Since you are left on your own concerning system security, you must develop your own approach (see Section 5.1) and focus on the types of passwords built into the accounting systems that are demonstrated to you. The approach for a hard disk system must be different from that for a diskette system.

For the hard disk system, you will have all of your various programs and data stored in the computer all of the time. If you do not set up some controls, anyone can turn on the computer and use the operating system to look at, alter, or destroy any information in there. The two most common operating systems are CP/M and MS/DOS. Neither of these have a password system built in. As a result, some new products have appeared that enhance the operating systems by adding password systems. Hopefully, the operating systems will be upgraded soon, so you won't have to add such enhancements. (It costs about $300 for a good one.)

The first password possible in a hard disk system is one requested every time the computer is turned on, regardless of what program the user intends to use. Related to this are passwords requested when changing from one program area to another in the computer's storage (from word processing to accounting, for example). Each password can also indicate whether that particular user can alter information or just read it without changing it. So you could set the system up to let one user read, add, or change information in the word processing area, yet prevent that user from seeing anything in the accounting area. Another user could be limited to looking at accounting information; for example, an order entry person checking the credit of potential customers.

A diskette-based system (without a hard disk) will only run a program when the user loads it into the computer. When the computer is turned off, that program disappears from its memory. If each program diskette has a password system built into its programs, then those diskettes carry their own protection. If the program on the diskette has no password system, it is not as secure. A good library system (see Section 5.2) will control access to the diskettes, but once someone is using one of the diskettes, there is nothing to stop the user from making copies (which will remain outside the library system).

The password systems built into accounting programs only control the use of the accounting system, not the access to its various stored files through some other program. Some offer password protection only at the first entrance into the program; once past that, the operator is free to carry out any accounting operation. You will have much better control with a two-level password system. This can be done in several ways.

One way is to have one additional password, the executive or manager password. Certain operations require this password, such as deleting account numbers, altering account balances, or setting up new passwords. We have seen one package that uses a simple code for this that cannot be changed, and it is mentioned throughout the user's manual. Anyone who has looked at that brand's manual would know the executive password. That is not very effective security. Another design error we have seen is to include the backup operations and/or the month-end closings with the privileged operations. That means that either you (the system manager) will have to come in and carry out the backup every day, or the operators will have to know the second-level password.

The second way to have multiple-level passwords is to assign a different password to each different accounting operation. Usually you only set such passwords on the functions you want protected; the rest you can leave accessible. With this method only the operators who know the password for printing checks, for example, will be able to do so. Each operator may have to memorize several different passwords, and when someone leaves the company, several passwords may need to be changed.

Some accounting systems let you set a unique password for each user, then have you select which functions that password will gain access to. With this method, each user you have assigned to print checks will be able to do so, even though they each have a different password. Each user has to know only one password. When someone leaves, you delete that password, and the other operators will not have to memorize new passwords.

On larger computer systems, this last method is commonly used. In addition, the activities of each operator are timed and monitored by the computer as it is used. No microcomputer is capable of this yet.

Only you and perhaps one other person should know the password needed to set, change, or look at passwords. You should write it down, along with any other private information about the system, and save it somewhere off the premises (such as a safe-deposit box). If you have assigned someone else as the system manager, you should insist on receiving a copy of this information and any changes made later.

Data security pertains to the fragility of your stored company information. A fluctuation in your electricity lines can instantly turn the information in your computer system into useless nonsense. Coffee and/or peanut butter on a diskette will usually do the same, and the contaminant can be transferred by the computer onto other diskettes used subsequently (such as your backup copies!). Such things do not happen often, but it only takes once to create a disaster. With a good set of backup and recovery procedures (see Section 5.3), however, you will be able to sleep soundly at night, assured that you are prepared for any possibility.

We do not consider the backup provisions of most systems adequate for accounting purposes. Most systems explain how many copies to make and when, but most then refer you to your operating system to carry out the operation. The operating system commands are tricky to use and hard to memorize. This is once again a do-it-yourself approach, leading to errors that could be easily avoided with more help from the accounting software. Another effect of this approach is that operators tend to back up the data less frequently. Any way to make it easier or more automatic will result in a more secure system.

Try the backup operation for each system you are considering buying. Have it explained by the dealer if it is not clear in the manual. You or your operators will have to back up after every data entry session, and it is very important to produce an accurate, complete set of data every time. If the operation is too confusing or cumbersome, ask the dealer to create a batch file that will automate the process for you. With MS/DOS systems it is a simple procedure, and it will save you and your operators much grief.

Recovery is the operation that you will carry out, by using your backup data, after an accident has interfered with your accounting system. Look for discussions of recovery procedures that go beyond which keys to push. You will need to know the possible consequences of your various options and develop a procedure that will minimize data losses. If you can find such a discussion, it is a good indication that the function has been well designed. The only way to be sure is to go through a realistic enactment (much like a fire drill) of a data loss and recovery.

The accounting aspects of security also involve maintaining the integrity of the data, not in a physical sense but in a systems analysis sense. This means you must ask what assurances you have that the correct processing has taken place and that the results reported to you are indeed what they are represented to be. Everyone tends to trust a computer's reports. This comes from when all computers were untouchable, operated and tended exclusively by experts. Today's micro systems do not fit that scenario at all; they are seldom operated by experts, and they are easily accessed by just about anyone.

Over the centuries accountants have developed systems that will notify you of most types of errors and will also help locate the errors. Those systems become even more important when a computer is used because so much can happen with no outward sign of trouble. Just as with a manual accounting system, each result reported should be traceable, step by step, back to the original document and forward again. These links are known as audit trails. And just as with the manual system, your accounting system should always remain in balance.

One example of an audit trail in a PC is the assigning of unique numbers to every transaction entered into the computer, along with an automatic logging of all changes and deletions. A printout of the transaction list and the changes and deletions log will provide a complete record of all input activity. A more common method of providing this same audit trail is for the system to force a printing of all of the transactions entered each time you post transactions to the ledger. Not only does this slow down the data entry process, but you can also end up with many different reports to shuffle through when looking for one piece of information.

Posting references are (usually) the document numbers of originating documents, such as checks and invoices. The PC accounting system should request them as part of the data entry information and include them on all of the appropriate reports. They are the trails from the reported transactions to the supporting documents.

Another audit trail tracks the printing of reports. It is common to print a report several times, going back and making adjustments each time until a final version is achieved. A problem arises here because you often end up with several reports that are almost identical, and you can easily be confused as to which report is which. If the system can assign sequential numbers to reports or can print the date and time on each one, then the trail is documented and the chance of error greatly reduced.

The computer system should not let your books get out of balance. This is easily accomplished by having the computer refuse to post any transaction or set of transactions that do not themselves balance. But many of the systems will allow out-of-balance situations; if so, they should constantly and prominently display a notice that the system is out of balance. Look out for any system that fails to do even that. We have seen some throw in a few numbers of their own when we printed a balance sheet in an out-of-balance situation so they appeared to be balanced! If balancing is forced like that, you cannot trust any of the numbers on the report because you don't have any idea which are correct and which have been changed.

Some final accounting security features are batch totaling, not allowing deletions of accounts that have ever had any activity, and not allowing changes to account balances without storing a record of such changes. A batch totaling system keeps a running total of many of the numbers entered into the computer, including numbers that do not represent dollar amounts, such as account numbers.

The concept is that the operator first uses an adding machine to run totals of those numbers for the batch to be entered, then when the entry into the computer has been completed, the adding machine tapes can be compared to the running totals the computer has kept. If the totals match, you can be fairly sure that all of the numbers were entered into the computer correctly.

Summary of What to Look For

General ledger

Flexibility is the most important aspect of a good general ledger program. Even if you are planning to transfer another area of your accounting to the computer before the general ledger (such as accounts receivable), you should familiarize yourself with the general ledger module first. It should allow you to use your company's existing chart of accounts. A flexible general ledger module will also allow you to design the format of your company's financial statements in the way that is most useful to you.

Support

The instruction manual(s) should include a complete tutorial, avoid programming jargon, and provide easy access to a reference section. A complete tutorial has the user set up a sample mini-company from the beginning through the first closing.

Ease of use

The use of microcomputer software includes the setup and the day-by-day use. The setup is invariably difficult, but some packages ease it significantly. Others make it into a real trial-and-error struggle. This is partly a function of the documentation. The day-by-day ease is more a function of the program's design. Some flow smoothly, but some are slow, cluttered, or just awkward.

Reports

The reports must be uncluttered yet complete. Desired detail should be possible on supplementary schedules. You should be able to design the reports to include what you want to see, including budgets and comparative statements.

Security

Three aspects of security are important here: password systems, backups, and complete audit trails. The passwords may be unnecessary in a very small business, but the other two are always important.

3.7 REQUIREMENTS/EVALUATION LISTS

We have talked about determining your needs before entering the micro marketplace as a serious shopper. In this section we present you with a set of lists that will guide you through this task—Figures 3.6 through 3.10. There is a list for each of the standard modules and one for those features that are important to all of the modules. These lists do not cover every detail and facet of accounting and computer systems; that would defeat their usefulness. They include the important features most small businesses should consider. Your particular situation or preferences may call for changes or additions.

These lists will serve several useful purposes. First, use them to organize your description of your current system as you analyze it. Second, note on that description the changes you plan to make and then mark every item as "required," "desired," or "don't care." Finally, use them to evaluate each accounting software package that is presented to you. This will make your evaluations consistent and ensure that all of your requirements and desires have been considered.

A set of more detailed lists, if desired, can be found in *The Software Sifter*, listed in Appendix B.

FIGURE 3.6

REQUIREMENTS/EVALUATION LIST—OVERALL SYSTEM

Support	**R***	**D***	**DC***
1. Evaluation			
a. can find the information needed	[ ]	[ ]	[ ]
b. sample reports provided	[ ]	[ ]	[ ]
c. current users to talk to	[ ]	[ ]	[ ]
2. Demonstrations satisfactory	[ ]	[ ]	[ ]
3. Tutorials and sample data adequate	[ ]	[ ]	[ ]
4. Manuals clear, complete, easy to use	[ ]	[ ]	[ ]
5. Training provided			
a. on computer use	[ ]	[ ]	[ ]
b. on accounting software	[ ]	[ ]	[ ]
6. After-sales support: Who provides it? At what costs?			
a. local dealer	[ ]	[ ]	[ ]
b. regional distributor	[ ]	[ ]	[ ]
c. software publisher	[ ]	[ ]	[ ]
7. Returns policy	[ ]	[ ]	[ ]
Ease of Use			
8. Are the setup instructions clear?	[ ]	[ ]	[ ]
9. Rate the data entry/posting operations (try it!)	[ ]	[ ]	[ ]
10. Rate the backing up operations	[ ]	[ ]	[ ]
11. Are the end-of-period closing instructions/demo. clear?	[ ]	[ ]	[ ]

FIGURE 3.6 (con.)

REQUIREMENTS/EVALUATION LIST—OVERALL SYSTEM

Features	R*	D*	DC*
12. Number of accounting periods (per year):______	[ ]	[ ]	[ ]
13. Can start new period before closing the old period	[ ]	[ ]	[ ]
14. Printer size:			
a. number of columns required:_____	[ ]	[ ]	[ ]
b. supports compressed characters mode	[ ]	[ ]	[ ]
15. Can transfer accounting data to spreadsheet or database program?			
16. List any exceptional features desired.			
Security			
17. Describe the access controls for the PC system. (in detail or satisfactory/unsatisfactory, as desired)			
18. Describe the access controls for the accounting operations.			
19. Batch system?	[ ]	[ ]	[ ]
20. Allows editing/deletions			
a. of active account numbers	[ ]	[ ]	[ ]
b. of active account balances	[ ]	[ ]	[ ]
c. of posted transactions	[ ]	[ ]	[ ]
21. Allows out-of-balance condition	[ ]	[ ]	[ ]
Long-Term Considerations			
22. List the computers and operating systems it will run on. (Will this limit your expansion options later?)			
23. Third-party support, both programmers and developers of hardware accessories—this is an indication of acceptance and thus compatibility with future developments.			

* R = Required
* D = Desired
* DC = Don't Care

FIGURE 3.7

REQUIREMENTS/EVALUATION LIST—GENERAL LEDGER

Capacities	R*	D*	DC*
1. Account number structure:			
a. alphanumeric	[ ]	[ ]	[ ]
b. number of digits in main account number: ______	[ ]	[ ]	[ ]
c. number of subaccount (department) digits: ______	[ ]	[ ]	[ ]
d. number of characters in description: ______	[ ]	[ ]	[ ]
2. Number of accounts in your chart of accounts: ______	[ ]	[ ]	[ ]
a. number range of assets		______ to ______	
b. number range of liabilities		______ to ______	
c. number range of equity accounts		______ to ______	
d. number range of income accounts		______ to ______	
e. number range of cost of goods sold		______ to ______	
f. number range of expenses		______ to ______	
3. Number of journal entries:			
a. per batch: ______	[ ]	[ ]	[ ]
b. per period: ______	[ ]	[ ]	[ ]
4. Number of companies to be handled: ______	[ ]	[ ]	[ ]
5. Number of departments to be handled: ______	[ ]	[ ]	[ ]
6. Number of journals to be handled: ______	[ ]	[ ]	[ ]
7. Maximum transaction amount			$______
8. Maximum total amount to be handled			$______

Reports	R*	D*	DC*
9. Types of statements desired:			
a. balance sheet	[ ]	[ ]	[ ]
b. balance sheet with prior year comparisons	[ ]	[ ]	[ ]
c. income statement	[ ]	[ ]	[ ]
d. income statement with departmental income statement	[ ]	[ ]	[ ]
e. income statement with monthly budget comparisons	[ ]	[ ]	[ ]

FIGURE 3.7 (con.)

REQUIREMENTS/EVALUATION LIST—GENERAL LEDGER

Reports	**R***	**D***	**DC***
f. income statement with prior year comparisons	[ ]	[ ]	[ ]
g. statement of changes in financial position	[ ]	[ ]	[ ]
h. subsidiary schedules to financial statements (for additional details)	[ ]	[ ]	[ ]
i. other custom reports	[ ]	[ ]	[ ]
10. Number of different formats desired for each financial statement:______	[ ]	[ ]	[ ]
11. Additional special reports or schedules desired	[ ]	[ ]	[ ]
12. Flexibility:			
a. formats fixed	[ ]	[ ]	[ ]
b. formats by assigning each account a type	[ ]	[ ]	[ ]
c. allows multiple formats	[ ]	[ ]	[ ]
13. Chart of accounts printout fits your needs	[ ]	[ ]	[ ]
14. Trial balance worksheet format meets your needs	[ ]	[ ]	[ ]
15. General ledger:			
a. format meets your needs	[ ]	[ ]	[ ]
b. separate report for each period	[ ]	[ ]	[ ]
c. multi-period detail in one report	[ ]	[ ]	[ ]
16. Reports displayed or printed:			
a. all go only to printer	[ ]	[ ]	[ ]
b. individual account inquiries to screen	[ ]	[ ]	[ ]
c. some reports to screen	[ ]	[ ]	[ ]
d. any report can be displayed to screen	[ ]	[ ]	[ ]
Features			
17. Accounting basis:			
a. cash	[ ]	[ ]	[ ]
b. accrual	[ ]	[ ]	[ ]
18. Number of capital accounts possible	[ ]	[ ]	[ ]

FIGURE 3.7 (con.)

REQUIREMENTS/EVALUATION LIST—GENERAL LEDGER

Features	R*	D*	DC*
19. Automatic posting of recurring entries (e.g., depreciation)	[ ]	[ ]	[ ]
20. Automatic allocation of expenses	[ ]	[ ]	[ ]
21. Automatic reversing of journal entries	[ ]	[ ]	[ ]
22. Correcting entries postable			
a. to prior period	[ ]	[ ]	[ ]
b. to prior year	[ ]	[ ]	[ ]
23. List any exceptional features.			

* R = Required
* D = Desired
* DC = Don't Care

FIGURE 3.8

REQUIREMENTS/EVALUATION LIST—ACCOUNTS RECEIVABLE

Capacities	R*	D*	DC*
1. Customer number structure:			
a. alphanumeric	[ ]	[ ]	[ ]
b. number of digits in customer body:______	[ ]	[ ]	[ ]
c. number of characters in description:______	[ ]	[ ]	[ ]
2. Other customer information to be accumulated	[ ]	[ ]	[ ]
3. Number of accounts receivable control accounts in your general ledger:______	[ ]	[ ]	[ ]
4. Number of general ledger accounts referenced by the accounts receivable module:______	[ ]	[ ]	[ ]
5. Number of recurring entries:______	[ ]	[ ]	[ ]

(con.)

FIGURE 3.8 (con.)

REQUIREMENTS/EVALUATION LIST—ACCOUNTS RECEIVABLE

Capacities	R*	D*	DC*
6. Number of one-time customers per period:______ (cash sales and miscellaneous receipts)	[ ]	[ ]	[ ]
7. Number of customers to whom you extend credit:______	[ ]	[ ]	[ ]
8. Number of invoices			
a. per batch:______	[ ]	[ ]	[ ]
b. per period:______	[ ]	[ ]	[ ]
9. Number of invoice payments			
a. per batch:______	[ ]	[ ]	[ ]
b. per period:______	[ ]	[ ]	[ ]
10. Maximum transaction amount			$______
11. Maximum total amount to be handled			$______
12. Number of lines per invoice:______	[ ]	[ ]	[ ]
13. Number of lines per statement:______	[ ]	[ ]	[ ]
Reports			
14. Aging report:			
a. summary	[ ]	[ ]	[ ]
b. detail	[ ]	[ ]	[ ]
c. all customers	[ ]	[ ]	[ ]
d. past-due customers	[ ]	[ ]	[ ]
e. sorted/selected by other criteria (e.g., amount)	[ ]	[ ]	[ ]
f. on-screen inquiries	[ ]	[ ]	[ ]
15. Customer roster:			
a. alphabetical	[ ]	[ ]	[ ]
b. numerical	[ ]	[ ]	[ ]
c. other (by zip code, etc.)	[ ]	[ ]	[ ]
d. mailing labels	[ ]	[ ]	[ ]

FIGURE 3.8 (con.)

REQUIREMENTS/EVALUATION LIST—ACCOUNTS RECEIVABLE

Reports	R*	D*	DC*
16. Prints invoices	[ ]	[ ]	[ ]
a. extends amounts	[ ]	[ ]	[ ]
b. calculates sales tax	[ ]	[ ]	[ ]
c. ship-to address	[ ]	[ ]	[ ]
17. Statements	[ ]	[ ]	[ ]
a. suppresses those with zero balances	[ ]	[ ]	[ ]
b. messages possible	[ ]	[ ]	[ ]
18. Sales analysis:			
a. by sales representative	[ ]	[ ]	[ ]
b. by sales territory	[ ]	[ ]	[ ]
19. Summary journal entries	[ ]	[ ]	[ ]
20. Detail journal entries	[ ]	[ ]	[ ]
21. Customer ledger	[ ]	[ ]	[ ]
Features			
22. Receivable types:			
a. open item (payment against specific invoices)	[ ]	[ ]	[ ]
b. balance forward (payments against balance)	[ ]	[ ]	[ ]
c. can be changed easily at any time	[ ]	[ ]	[ ]
23. Aging periods:			
a. selectable	[ ]	[ ]	[ ]
b. including future amounts due	[ ]	[ ]	[ ]
24. Automatic posting of recurring charges	[ ]	[ ]	[ ]
25. Credit memos	[ ]	[ ]	[ ]
26. Debit memos	[ ]	[ ]	[ ]
27. Finance charges	[ ]	[ ]	[ ]
a. with compounding	[ ]	[ ]	[ ]

FIGURE 3.8 (con.)

REQUIREMENTS/EVALUATION LIST—ACCOUNTS RECEIVABLE

Features	R*	D*	DC*
28. Discounts	[ ]	[ ]	[ ]
29. Partial payments	[ ]	[ ]	[ ]
30. Credit limit checking	[ ]	[ ]	[ ]
31. Cash sales and miscellaneous receipts	[ ]	[ ]	[ ]
32. Sales commissions computed	[ ]	[ ]	[ ]
a. number of different rates	[ ]	[ ]	[ ]
33. Late charges	[ ]	[ ]	[ ]
34. List any exceptional features.			

* R = Required
* D = Desired
* DC = Don't Care

FIGURE 3.9

REQUIREMENTS/EVALUATION LIST—ACCOUNTS PAYABLE

Capacities	R*	D*	DC*
1. Vendor number structure:			
a. alphanumeric	[ ]	[ ]	[ ]
b. number of digits in vendor number:______	[ ]	[ ]	[ ]
c. number of characters in description:______	[ ]	[ ]	[ ]
2. Other vendor information to be accumulated	[ ]	[ ]	[ ]
3. Number of accounts payable control accounts in your general ledger:______	[ ]	[ ]	[ ]
4. Number of general ledger control accounts referenced by the accounts payable module:______	[ ]	[ ]	[ ]
5. Number of recurring entries:______	[ ]	[ ]	[ ]
6. Number of one-time vendors per period:______	[ ]	[ ]	[ ]

FIGURE 3.9 (con.)

REQUIREMENTS/EVALUATION LIST—ACCOUNTS PAYABLE

Capacities	R*	D*	DC*
7. Number of invoices			
a. per batch: _______	[ ]	[ ]	[ ]
b. per period: _______	[ ]	[ ]	[ ]
8. Number of checks			
a. per batch: _______	[ ]	[ ]	[ ]
b. per period: _______	[ ]	[ ]	[ ]
9. Number of checking accounts: _______	[ ]	[ ]	[ ]
10. Maximum invoice amount			$_______
11. Maximum total amount to be handled			$_______
12. Number of lines per voucher description (The voucher is the portion on the check where the invoice number and description is written.): _______	[ ]	[ ]	[ ]
Reports			
13. Aging reports:			
a. summary	[ ]	[ ]	[ ]
b. detail	[ ]	[ ]	[ ]
c. all vendors	[ ]	[ ]	[ ]
d. selected vendors	[ ]	[ ]	[ ]
e. by due date	[ ]	[ ]	[ ]
f. by amount owed	[ ]	[ ]	[ ]
g. by other	[ ]	[ ]	[ ]
h. future amounts due	[ ]	[ ]	[ ]
i. on-screen inquiries	[ ]	[ ]	[ ]
14. Vendor roster:			
a. alphabetical	[ ]	[ ]	[ ]
b. numerical	[ ]	[ ]	[ ]
c. mailing labels	[ ]	[ ]	[ ]
15. Payment selection listing	[ ]	[ ]	[ ]

FIGURE 3.9 (con.)

REQUIREMENTS/EVALUATION LIST—ACCOUNTS PAYABLE

Reports	R*	D*	DC*
16. Checks	[ ]	[ ]	[ ]
a. inhibits zero and negative amounts	[ ]	[ ]	[ ]
b. check "protector" pattern	[ ]	[ ]	[ ]
17. Check register	[ ]	[ ]	[ ]
a. flags breaks in the number sequence	[ ]	[ ]	[ ]
b. lists manually prepared checks	[ ]	[ ]	[ ]
c. notes voided checks	[ ]	[ ]	[ ]
18. Outstanding checks listing	[ ]	[ ]	[ ]
19. Discounts lost	[ ]	[ ]	[ ]
20. Vendor analysis	[ ]	[ ]	[ ]
21. Summary journal entries	[ ]	[ ]	[ ]
22. Detail journal entries	[ ]	[ ]	[ ]
23. Vendor ledger	[ ]	[ ]	[ ]
Features			
24. Payment selection options (who to pay):			
a. by vendor name	[ ]	[ ]	[ ]
b. by vendor number	[ ]	[ ]	[ ]
c. by due date	[ ]	[ ]	[ ]
d. by aging	[ ]	[ ]	[ ]
e. by invoice number	[ ]	[ ]	[ ]
f. by exception (pay all except. . .)	[ ]	[ ]	[ ]
25. Hold payment(s) option	[ ]	[ ]	[ ]
26. Reverse an invoice previously selected for payment	[ ]	[ ]	[ ]
27. Voided checks			
a. computer prepared	[ ]	[ ]	[ ]
b. manually prepared	[ ]	[ ]	[ ]

FIGURE 3.9 (con.)

REQUIREMENTS/EVALUATION LIST—ACCOUNTS PAYABLE

Features	R*	D*	DC*
28. Recurring checks	[ ]	[ ]	[ ]
29. Credit memos	[ ]	[ ]	[ ]
30. Debit memos	[ ]	[ ]	[ ]
31. Finance charges	[ ]	[ ]	[ ]
32. Discounts	[ ]	[ ]	[ ]
33. Discounts forced (past discount date)	[ ]	[ ]	[ ]
34. Partial payments	[ ]	[ ]	[ ]
35. Manually prepared checks	[ ]	[ ]	[ ]
36. One-time-only checks	[ ]	[ ]	[ ]
37. List any exceptional features.			

* R = Required
* D = Desired
* DC = Don't Care

FIGURE 3.10

REQUIREMENTS/EVALUATION LIST—PAYROLL

Capacities	R*	D*	DC*
1. Employee account number structure:			
a. alphanumeric	[ ]	[ ]	[ ]
b. number of digits in employee account number:______	[ ]	[ ]	[ ]
2. Employee information to be accumulated	[ ]	[ ]	[ ]
3. Number of payroll accounts in your general ledger:______	[ ]	[ ]	[ ]
4. Number of general ledger accounts referenced by the payroll module:______	[ ]	[ ]	[ ]
5. Number of permanent employees:______	[ ]	[ ]	[ ]

FIGURE 3.10 (con.)

REQUIREMENTS/EVALUATION LIST—PAYROLL

Capacities	R*	D*	DC*
6. Types of pay period(s) (semimonthly, etc.)	[ ]	[ ]	[ ]
7. Maximum paycheck amount			$_______
8. Maximum total amount to be handled			$_______
9. Maximum number of employees:_______	[ ]	[ ]	[ ]
10. Number of optional deductions:_______	[ ]	[ ]	[ ]
Reports			
11. Checks:			
a. fixed format	[ ]	[ ]	[ ]
b. flexible format	[ ]	[ ]	[ ]
12. Check register	[ ]	[ ]	[ ]
13. Employee roster	[ ]	[ ]	[ ]
14. Employee inquiry (all details)	[ ]	[ ]	[ ]
15. Wage reports (individual employee compensation records)	[ ]	[ ]	[ ]
16. Payroll summary	[ ]	[ ]	[ ]
17. Pre-check-printing report	[ ]	[ ]	[ ]
18. 1099s	[ ]	[ ]	[ ]
19. 941s	[ ]	[ ]	[ ]
20. W2s	[ ]	[ ]	[ ]
21. Checks	[ ]	[ ]	[ ]
a. inhibits zero and negative amounts	[ ]	[ ]	[ ]
b. check "protector" pattern	[ ]	[ ]	[ ]
22. Check register	[ ]	[ ]	[ ]
a. flags breaks in the number sequence	[ ]	[ ]	[ ]
b. lists manually prepared checks	[ ]	[ ]	[ ]
c. notes voided checks	[ ]	[ ]	[ ]

FIGURE 3.10 (con.)

REQUIREMENTS/EVALUATION LIST—PAYROLL

Reports	R*	D*	DC*
23. Summary journal entries	[ ]	[ ]	[ ]
24. Detail journal entries	[ ]	[ ]	[ ]
25. Outstanding checks listing	[ ]	[ ]	[ ]
Features			
26. Payroll types:			
a. hourly	[ ]	[ ]	[ ]
b. salaried	[ ]	[ ]	[ ]
c. commission	[ ]	[ ]	[ ]
d. other	[ ]	[ ]	[ ]
27. Supplemental pay:			
a. holiday	[ ]	[ ]	[ ]
b. vacation	[ ]	[ ]	[ ]
c. sick time	[ ]	[ ]	[ ]
d. other	[ ]	[ ]	[ ]
28. Manually prepared checks	[ ]	[ ]	[ ]
29. Voided checks			
a. computer prepared	[ ]	[ ]	[ ]
b. manually prepared	[ ]	[ ]	[ ]
30. Automatic deductions:			
a. union fees	[ ]	[ ]	[ ]
b. loans	[ ]	[ ]	[ ]
c. garnishments	[ ]	[ ]	[ ]
d. health insurance	[ ]	[ ]	[ ]
e. other	[ ]	[ ]	[ ]
31. Worker's compensation calculations	[ ]	[ ]	[ ]
32. Terminated employees	[ ]	[ ]	[ ]
33. Inactive employees	[ ]	[ ]	[ ]
34. Pay advances	[ ]	[ ]	[ ]

FIGURE 3.10 (con.)

REQUIREMENTS/EVALUATION LIST—PAYROLL

Features	R*	D*	DC*
35. Withholding tables:			
a. entered and maintained by user	[ ]	[ ]	[ ]
b. supplied and updated by software publisher	[ ]	[ ]	[ ]
36. List any exceptional features.			

* R = Required
* D = Desired
* DC = Don't Care

4

THE CONVERSION PROCESS

4.1 INTRODUCTION

Even after you have decided to computerize, have selected an appropriate system, and have purchased it, you are only halfway there. You cannot just pop in a diskette and print out a receivables aging report. There are a couple of intermediate steps that have to be done first: the software installation and the conversion process. The installation is the process of putting the software and hardware together. The conversion consists of gathering and entering data, training personnel, and testing. This must be done for each accounting module you have selected.

The difficulty of the installation varies with different accounting packages, but the dealer you purchase it from should agree to install it for you. After that, the key to a smooth transition is planning—how and when to input the setup information, how and when to get the people involved, and anticipating the impact that the conversion process itself will have on your busy staff.

This chapter on the conversion process assumes you are not using a consultant. If you are using a consultant to help with your conversion, you will not need to do some of the studying and learning steps. Your consultant will have gone through enough conversions to have learned the best way to proceed and will advise you on schedules, information and training requirements, and labor resource requirements.

4.2 LEARNING THE SOFTWARE

Before you can make the proper planning decisions for your conversion, you need to know what you are getting into. You must have a thorough understanding of the entire software package and how its various elements work together. All of today's complex computer programs (not just accounting) seem to require some trial-and-error experimentation by a new user. Various secrets of the package continue to be discovered for weeks or months, depending on how heavily and powerfully it is used. Most of these additional features are documented somewhere in the manuals, but they cannot all be learned at once.

Because of the repetition, the procedures that you use often are normally the first ones that you learn. This works fairly well for word processing or spreadsheet programs; a new user can start out with the basic operations and, over time, work up to the more advanced features.

This does not work with accounting packages. With these, you must do a complex setup at the very start, using all of the appropriate advanced features of the programs. You are not allowed to gradually learn additional features as time goes by. If you don't build a certain feature in at the onset, you probably will not be able to use it until 12 months go by, if then. This is a major reason that so many businesses end up going through the setup of their computerized accounting system several times before they achieve a satisfactory result.

The solution is not simply to ask for manuals that are well written, in plain English, and that contain all of the information you might need. That would still require the new user to have enormous learning capacity and motivation, because of the sheer quantity of information involved. It is difficult to conceive of a manual that would specifically cover the needs of all the different types of uses and users.

Computer software manuals have improved rapidly over the past few years, as new products and generations of products were developed. But accounting software requires that special conversion process, where you take the general package and set it up for your specific business. Neither the software nor the manuals address that task adequately. Many do not discuss it at all.

So the first part of your preparation for conversion is to sit down with the manuals and do some studying. You will have to sift through the manuals to find out how and when to do the different procedures we outline in Section 4.3 of this book. There are certain to be items that you cannot find in the manual. Often there is no index to help you, and sometimes the information simply isn't included in the manual.

Your dealer is the first place to look for answers to these points. Also, some brands of accounting software have set up additional support facilities for their end-users. Check to see if they provide a telephone number to call for answers. Some will offer it free, some will charge for such support, and others refuse to talk to end-users. In the latter case, try harder to maintain good terms with your dealer, because you may have nowhere else to turn for help. One way to ease the relationship is to not call every time a new question comes up; rather, accumulate a list of questions. That way neither of you will become as frustrated. The dealer won't be interrupted constantly, and you won't always be waiting for a return call.

If you do find yourself having problems this soon, without satisfactory responses from the dealer or the software house, think again about having a consultant help. It is difficult for a consultant to come in after months of struggle and attempt to complete your conversion. By that time the personnel are no longer receptive, and the alternatives are often limited, either by budget restrictions or by poor dealer relationships. So if you are already having problems at the planning stage, it is time to reconsider getting help.

If you find the documentation and the support satisfactory for planning your conversion, then you are well on your way to having it accomplished.

4.3 PLANNING AND SCHEDULING

This section starts by discussing some general aspects of preparing for your conversion and offers some thoughts about which accounting function to convert first. Then it presents the nine phases you will go through to convert each module.

Getting Ready

A prerequisite for your conversion is to have your books in good order. They should be maintained on a consistent time schedule, such as monthly or quarterly, and be in balance. Cash, accounts receivable, inventory, and so on, should each be supported by a reconciliation to the balance in the general ledger.

This is the time for you to consider making improvements or changes in your accounting system. As you study each software module in preparation for the conversion, look at the structures and features built into it, and note those that are especially appropriate or inappropriate for your business. Look beyond the initial statement of a feature, and see how it affects the results. For example, even though the program can be set up to work with your current three-digit vendor numbers, it may not list the vendors in alphabetical order unless you change your vendor numbers to codes that consist of two letters followed by three numbers.

Most accounting programs now allow any number of

general ledger accounts, so you can easily expand your chart of accounts to provide more detail where desired. Then, with a little additional effort by your accounting staff, far more variety and focus will be available for management reports.

If you can convert to the computerized system as of the beginning of your fiscal year, it will be easier. Usually a great deal of work has been done for the year-end, getting ready for the preparation of financial statements and tax returns. This puts the books into especially good order for the conversion. Since that is the only time of the year when all of the income and expense accounts have zeros as beginning balances, there is also less data entry required. There tends to be less accounting to do at the beginning of an accounting period, particularly if the low point of the business cycle is timed to coincide with the end of the fiscal year. This means more availability of your accounting staff for the extra work of the conversion.

Which Module First?

Often one area of your accounting gives you the most problems, and you view it as the most important area to computerize. For example, if cash flow is a problem, then converting the accounts receivable can provide a more efficient billing system. This can lead to earlier collections of receivables, easing the cash situation. But you shouldn't automatically decide to convert your worst problem area first. Starting with the general ledger module has many advantages.

The general ledger is the easiest and fastest conversion in most cases. It also stands the greatest chance of success on the first try. The data needed for the conversion is usually readily available; it comes from a single source and does not have to be assembled. There is usually less data to be entered and fewer transactions per accounting period.

After you have experienced what is involved in a relatively simple conversion, you are better prepared for the areas that are more important and complicated. Because the interactions between modules revolve around the general ledger account numbers, you can also be more assured that the various modules will interact properly when you are ready for that final step.

The Steps to a Conversion

There are nine general phases to the conversion of each accounting module. They are:

1. Study your current system
2. Design the new system
3. Set up the software structure
4. Gather and organize the data
5. Enter and verify the data
6. Operator training
7. System testing and startup
8. Integration between modules
9. Final documentation of procedures

The remainder of Chapter 4 discusses each of these phases. In Section 4.12 you will develop a schedule for your conversions. Figures 4.1 through 4.4 are detailed conversion checklists for the four types of accounting modules.

4.4 DESIGNING THE NEW SYSTEM

You are designing your system when you are deciding such things as how your general ledger account numbers will be structured, what reports you want, and how those reports will look. You did most of the system design before you went to purchase the software and hardware, when you filled out the evaluation/requirements lists (Sections 2.3 and 3.7). This is one phase of the conversion where it is especially important that a professional accountant be involved.

For this phase of the conversion, you want to put your requirements lists together with the software and fill in the holes. Some of your requirements and wishes may not be available with the software you selected, and there will be some decisions to make that you hadn't considered (and may not care about). For example, the Great Plains accounting software supports certain color printers. You would only care about that if you were using such a printer, but you would still have to tell the software that you were not using colors.

At this point you should know which micro-accounting modules you plan on using. This is the time to design your password system, because it is a feature that encompasses all of those modules. Familiarize yourself with the types and levels of passwords available and how to set them up. Decide who will be doing each operation and which operations you alone should have access to (such as setting and changing passwords, and the system setup options).

You must write all of this password information down and store it in a safe place. You should not be the only one who knows where this information is kept. If you are the system manager for your company, then you can store the numbers in a safe-deposit box and tell some of the staff they are there. That way they normally will not have access to them, but if anything happens to you, the information is not lost.

If you feel strongly that you do not desire passwords to prevent unauthorized access, you should still set up some simple ones to prevent accidental activation of certain critical operations. It is very easy for new operators to accidentally type one wrong key and find themselves in unfamiliar territory. At that point the tendency is to try a few hopeful strategies before giving up and calling for help. In the password setup and the end-of-period processing operations, for example, this can result in new (and unknown) passwords or an unanticipated early closing of the accounting period. These things have actually happened.

The general ledger module requires a more extensive design phase than the other modules. The chart of accounts is the key to how the data will be accumulated. If you want more detail, then you will need to set up accounts to capture that detail. The journals will have to reflect your accounting system. If you are on a cash basis, you will need a cash receipts, cash disbursements, and general journal, among others. If you are on an accrual basis, you will need an accounts receivable, accounts payable, and general journal, among others.

This is where you should specify which types of financial statements you want and how you want them to look. Decide which accounts should be grouped together and what titles those summary figures should have. Sketch out each report on blank paper as you would like to see it.

For the other modules you will be converting, you made most of the design decisions when you selected the software. Now you only have to find out what other options the software will expect you to decide among. If the manual isn't clear about the software's options, you can usually run through the program's SETUP or INITIALIZATION operation using a practice diskette, just to see what questions are asked. Erase that diskette and start over when you are ready to carry out the actual setup.

4.5 SETTING UP THE SOFTWARE STRUCTURE

This phase of the conversion is intimately related to the system design phase, for it is the process of telling the software what design decisions you have made. This process should be done by the designer of the new system and not by a data entry operator. It is a one-time process and is critical to the success of the conversion.

Much of this operation is done almost automatically as you run the program's setup routine (the routine is called SETUP, INITIALIZATION, INSTALL, or something similar). This routine asks you a series of questions, and your answers determine how the system gets set up. The company name you supply here will be used by the system to identify reports; if you use all upper-case letters, then the reports will show all upper-case letters. You may be asked how many digits you will use for your account numbers. Some of these answers cannot be changed later without starting the conversion over again.

Not all of the structure is set up by answering the program's questions. The general ledger requires a lot of setting up. The chart of accounts has account numbers and descriptions to be entered into the computer. Most of these accounts will have balance forward amounts that must be entered so that the new system will initially balance with the old system. All of the report formatting information has to be entered into the computer.

Entering the chart of accounts is usually straightforward. The balance forward amounts are another matter. Some programs have special routines you use just for this purpose. Others expect you to make a special journal entry for each account. The special routines can usually be used only one time so that no one can go in later and alter those beginning balances.

The *formatting* for your financial statements is done differently by every program. All are difficult until you learn the rules. Some programs (including CYMA, MBSI, and Solomon III) allow many different formats to be created and stored, and allow you to edit them without starting from scratch. These are difficult at first, but after you learn the rules, the reports are easier to create.

Other programs allow just one format, and you construct that format as you enter your chart of accounts. If you are adding many new accounts, and especially if you are using departments for the first time, this can become a difficult exercise. You have to create many special "non-posting accounts" that have no purpose other than providing titles on reports, or else accumulating sums for the subtotals and totals shown on the reports.

The other modules generally require only that the program's questions be answered. You will have additional setup to do only if the invoices, statements, company checks, and/or paychecks have flexible formats for you to design.

4.6 GATHERING AND ORGANIZING DATA

Gather your data together and organize it before starting to enter it into the computer. The computer has been programmed to ask for the data in a certain sequence, and for the data entry portion of your setup, the sequence of questions will be repeated over and over. For example, when setting up an inventory program, the computer repeatedly asks for the part number, the part description, the vendor's part number, the unit of measure, the cost, the minimum quantity to keep on hand, and so on. It asks these questions once for each part until you tell it that all of your parts have been entered.

The computer industry learned long ago that errors during data entry are dramatically decreased if the data is gathered together beforehand so that the operator is not continually shuffling and searching for the next data item. An extreme illustration of this would be if the answers to the first question were in one file cabinet, the answers to the second were in a second file cabinet, and the answers to the third question had to be calculated before they were known. In this case it is clear that the data should be brought together and the calculations performed before even turning on the computer.

To do this, first list how your software requests the data: what form and in what order. Then locate those data items in your records, and note on the list where they are to be found. Finally, if the data is scattered, compile your data onto an appropriate DATA INPUT FORM for that data entry session.

These data input forms are not only for the entering of data. They are necessary for the verification of the data after it has all been entered. Also, they become a clear record of just what amounts were entered at the startup of the system, in case that needs to be checked at a later date.

Often there are appropriate input forms provided in the software manual. If the software manual doesn't describe its data input screens or the questions that will be asked, you can run the program just to get a look at the screens.

The closer the data input form is to the expected order of entry, the better, but there is a tradeoff in the amount of effort to get it there versus the improved speed and accuracy to be derived. You must consider the location, the identification, and the legibility of your current data. If you have a set of ledger cards with most of your data items on each card and two data items elsewhere, you may be able to just add the two numbers to each card, and then use the cards as the data input forms. However, if the cards are written illegibly or the different items are not clearly separated and identified, then they should be copied onto a new data input form (by the person best qualified to decipher the cards).

For the general ledger module, the only data to be entered by a clerk is that for monthly budgets or prior-year comparisons. For entering your budget amounts, prepare worksheets that list the 12 amounts for each account you are budgeting. If your program asks for the 12 amounts in a vertical list (most do), then you should format your data input sheets so the 12 amounts are arranged similarly rather than putting the months horizontally across the pages.

For entering the amounts for prior-year comparative reports, you will need a trial balance report for each month (or period) that you will want to compare. These reports make good data input forms.

Accounts receivable and payable conversions usually involve at least dozens, and often hundreds, of customers and vendors. In addition, any recurring receivables or payables are usually set up separately from the *master files* and are an additional data entry step. Since you want all of this data entry done correctly and accurately, you will need to develop a separate data input sheet for each customer and vendor, unless your data is already organized that way.

For the payroll module, it is the employee data that will be entered. If you have many employees, you will need to organize the data in preparation for typing it into the computer.

4.7 ENTERING YOUR INITIAL DATA

This phase is straightforward, but it can be a lengthy project, depending on the amount of data to be entered. You need to consider who should do the data entry and verifications, how long it will take, and how to oversee the process.

If your staff is fairly busy, they may not be the best choice for entering the data. This task will not enhance their knowledge of the accounting system, and an experienced data entry clerk will accomplish it much faster and with fewer mistakes. There are many agencies that specialize in supplying data entry personnel for this type of short-term project. Students from a nearby college campus are a more cost-effective alternative, but they are generally limited in the amount of time they can spend on the project during the school year. Also, their experience is likely to be limited.

For an idea of how long this process takes, consider the following actual experience in setting up an accounts receivable package. A business had slightly over 200 steady customers, most of them needing to be set up with two to four recurring entries. Using an experienced data entry clerk on a temporary basis, it took about a month to enter all the data. That included entering about 200 customers into the accounts receivable master files, entering about 500 recurring entries, and then verifying all of the data that had been entered. There was no need to compile the data beforehand because the accounts receivable were being kept by an outside computer service that could provide the data in the needed format.

This process needs to be overseen by someone knowledgeable about the accounting software used. Periodic checks are necessary to ensure that the data is going into the system correctly. It is also important to institute formal backup procedures for this data entry project and for the remainder of the conversion. This is the time when something is most likely to go wrong, with new users forgetting operations and much of the new system unknown. Every time a new operation is going to be tried, first make a copy (or two) of your data in the computer, just in case something doesn't work as expected (see Section 5.4 for more information on backing up).

4.8 OPERATOR TRAINING

For best results with your current staff, involve them early—as soon as you decide you are definitely going to computerize. The computer represents a major change in your operations, and many people will feel threatened by that. It is not enough to just say to them, "This is how it will be." And don't expect them to sit down and learn it themselves on their own time; they won't do it. You could encounter more resistance, and even sabotage, as a result.

It usually takes a long time before a new user begins to feel comfortable around the computer. A key factor here is motivation. When people buy PCs of their own, they are highly motivated to learn to use them. Such new users are often so enthusiastic that they are irritating to people not yet involved. Your staff has no such built-in motivation to help you through this; you must provide it. Most people respond positively to rewards, so you can show your people how the computer will enhance their jobs once they help you get it started up. It will do the less desirable aspects of their jobs, freeing them to do more fulfilling tasks.

Discussing how the computer will fit in will also reassure your staff that you don't intend to lay them all off when the conversion is completed. They will appreciate being told what is happening and what their part in the conversion is.

Arrange to give your employees formal training on the computer. Introductory computer classes are offered by computer stores, university extension classes, consultants, and companies that specialize in training new users of PCs. Also encourage your staff to play with and use the computer during the planning stages of the conversion, as part of their training. One way to do this is to use the tutorials provided in the user manuals that come with the software. You can also use your own records as a source of data to practice with. The use of some past months' records provides readily available answers with which to check the practice results. Be sure to formally schedule time for them to do this during working hours, or many of your employees won't get around to doing it.

Since there are generally no classes available that teach the accounting functions of specific software packages, you may want to set up some training sessions with a specialist who knows that subject. If you are bringing your accounting in-house from an outside accounting service, you probably have no one on your staff who knows how to distribute the different transactions to the proper accounts. The software does not do that step for you.

4.9 SYSTEM STARTUP AND TESTING

After entering the initial data, you are ready to start entering transactions in parallel with your old system. This means that each transaction should be entered in the same way in both systems, so they can be evaluated for comparable results. This involves duplication of effort, but it is necessary to test your new system sufficiently before relying on it. These parallel runs are typically done for two or three accounting periods.

At the completion of the first accounting period, print out the journal entry listings, the general ledger, and the financial statements. Compare these reports to the corresponding ones from your old system. Sometimes changes you made in the system design phase mean that certain transactions cannot be entered identically. In such cases the resulting reports will have to be adjusted to compensate for the differences between the two systems. For example, if you broke one old account into three new ones to get more detail, you will have to sum those three accounts to get the comparable amount.

There are usually discrepancies to be investigated at this point. When you have located the source of each problem, you can make the appropriate adjustments to the new system or to the accounting procedures involved. The second period of running in parallel may result in no discrepancies; if so, the third period may not be necessary.

It is not less work, but it is quicker to do the first two parallel runs over the last two months prior to conversion, instead of drawing it out over subsequent months. If the number of transactions is not prohibitive, this can be done in a couple of days on the new system, and then the reports can be compared immediately. You should still run in parallel for one month, but that should be sufficient if nothing is found amiss.

This is also the time when you are instituting the new standard operating procedures for your computerized system (discussed in Chapter 5). Remember that some of these procedures will change when you start up additional accounting modules and integrate them into the new system.

4.10 INTEGRATION OF MODULES

The integration of the accounting modules is deceptively easy: Just push a couple of buttons on the computer, and it's done. The question that must be asked is, "What is done?" It can be tricky trying to determine if the intermodule transactions are what they should be.

If you follow these steps, you can achieve a properly integrated system with a minimum of effort. First, have the modules involved running correctly in a stand-alone mode before integrating them. Then, make a duplicate copy of all of your accounting data and use the copy to practice the integration operation. Check the results. If they are not correct, you have lost nothing. You can make any number of these practice integrations until you arrive at a procedure that works. Document that procedure and test it one more time before you use it to integrate your live system.

4.11 FINAL DOCUMENTATION OF PROCEDURES

An important part of your conversion is the documentation of the procedures you develop. The manual that comes with the software is not the type of documentation you need for your operators in their day-to-day work. They will need step-by-step sequences written down for each of the various operations in your system. If you don't provide it, the operators will come up with their own, on various scraps of paper that only they know about. After a while the procedures will be learned, and these memory aids will not be used much, but they will continue to be valuable when you hire new people or when a key operator is out sick.

A good way to develop this documentation is to have a second person make notes as the daily and monthly operations are performed at the computer. Before these notes are compiled to be used, they should be tested by having someone follow them step by step and see if the results are as expected. It is handy to use a word processing program to generate this document because there are so many changes made to it over the first couple of months. For example, some of the procedures will change when you finally integrate the different modules.

It is also a good idea to insert into this document some notes concerning common or anticipated errors and how to recover from them. These will be readily evident to your operators at first, but as they gain experience on the system they will forget those initial problems and not warn new trainees about them. For example, a program's input screens may become scrambled by use of the backspace key. Of course, the software should not allow that, but that knowledge won't help users of that particular software. A new operator soon learns not to use the backspace key, but advance warning speeds this learning. Also, an explanation of what to do when it does happen can save the new operator time and unnecessary anguish.

4.12 CONVERSION CHECKLISTS

This section takes the nine phases and adds, in outline form, the detailed steps needed for each of the four types of accounting modules (see Figures 4.1 through 4.4). These outlines can be used for developing your schedule, and as checklists to monitor your progress during the actual conversion project.

To develop your schedule for converting your accounting system, use both the detailed lists of steps and the preceding discussions of each phase. The checklists help by showing the steps to be done and the order in which to do them. For each task on the lists, decide who will do it, and estimate how long it might take. Your estimates will depend on your business situation, on the level of your help (and their availability), and on your software.

After you have developed a schedule for the individual modules you will be converting, you should bring the whole project together and look at the overall time and labor requirements. This is especially important if you are planning to convert more than one module at a time, or with any overlap.

FIGURE 4.1 General Ledger Conversion Checklist

- I. Study current system.
  - A. See Section 2.3, "Accounting Needs."
- II. Design new system.
  - A. Design chart of accounts.
    1. What departments will be involved (e.g., locations, branches, cost centers, profit centers)?
    2. What level of detail is desired (e.g., multiple sales accounts to show categories of sales or just one overall sales account)?
    3. Rewrite chart of accounts to include any changes.
  - B. Design journals.
    1. What journals will be needed (e.g., cash receipts, cash disbursements, general journal)?

FIGURE 4.1 General Ledger Conversion Checklist (con.)

- C. Design reports.
  - 1. What types of reports are desired/needed?
    - a. chart of accounts
    - b. balance sheet
      - (1) balance sheet with prior-year comparisons
    - c. income statement
      - (1) income statement with departmental income statements
      - (2) income statement with monthly budget comparisons
      - (3) income statement with prior-year comparisons
    - d. statement of changes in financial position
    - e. subsidiary schedules to financial statements (for additional detail)
    - f. other custom reports
- D. Design password system.

III. Set up software structure (differs significantly between brands of software).
- A. Enter the new user information, such as company name and address, passwords, and sometimes type of printer, balance forward date, and so on.
- B. Enter the chart of accounts and balance forward amounts (You will need a trial balance as of the balance forward date for the general ledger).
- C. Enter the desired report formats (if your program allows this to be done separately from the data entry procedure).
- D. Verify all of the data entered by printing out and proofing the appropriate reports. For example, the chart of accounts, the general ledger, and the financial statements.
- E. Make corrections as necessary.

IV. Gather and organize data.
- A. For comparative reports, you will need a trial balance for each month (or quarter) that you will want to compare.
- B. For monthly budgets, you will need a worksheet showing the monthly budget amounts for each account involved.

V. Data entry and verification
- A. Use the above worksheets to enter the amounts.
- B. Print out the appropriate reports and verify the amounts against the original worksheets.
- C. Make corrections as necessary.

FIGURE 4.1 General Ledger Conversion Checklist (con.)

VI. Operator training (for day-to-day operations)
  A. Formal training
    1. Send employees to classes.
    2. Training sessions with specialist (who knows that accounting software and is familiar with your accounting system)
  B. Informal training
    1. Tutorials
    2. On-the-job training (from someone in the company who has been trained)
    3. Discussion groups (to answer questions, allay fears, describe benefits)

VII. System testing and startup
  A. Start entering transactions to appropriate journals, in parallel to your current system.
    1. At the completion of the first accounting period (usually a month), print the journal entry listings, the general ledger, and the financial statements, and compare them to the manual system.
    2. Locate the source of any discrepancies, and make adjustments.

VIII. Integration of modules
  A. Be sure that each additional module is running correctly in a stand-alone mode before integrating it into the rest of your system.
  B. Use an extra (duplicate diskette) copy of your accounting data (for the modules involved) to do a trial integration (i.e., do a parallel run to your computer system).
  C. Print out the appropriate reports and check the integration results.
  D. Locate the source of any problems, make adjustments, and try it again.
  E. Only when it is working correctly should you integrate your live system.

IX. Final documentation of your micro-accounting procedures
  A. As you start up your daily entry on the computer system, make notes as to how that entry is being performed. (step by step, in detail, plus notes on common or anticipated errors, and how to recover from them).
  B. Compile the notes on the various operations into an organized document.
  C. Test the document by carrying out (on the computer) every step listed.

FIGURE 4.2 Accounts Receivable Conversion Checklist

I. Study current system.
   A. See Section 2.3, "Accounting Needs."

II. Design new system.
   A. Decide which method of receivables accounting you will be using, balance forward or open item, or both.
   B. Determine what, if any, recurring entries will be needed.
   C. Design customer number.
   D. Determine what information is to be accumulated on each customer.
   E. Design format of invoices and statements, if applicable to your software.
   F. Order invoices and statements to fit the new system.
   G. Design password system.

III. Set up software structure (differs significantly between brands of software).
   A. Enter the new user information, such as company name and address, passwords, and sometimes type of printer, balance forward date, and so on.
   B. Enter the desired report formats (if applicable).
   C. Verify all of the data entered by printing out and proofing the appropriate reports.
   D. Make corrections as necessary.

IV. Gather and organize data.
   A. Determine the input form for setting up the receivables (what specific information, and the order it will be needed).
   B. Locate the data items and determine how much gathering and compiling will be needed. You want to end up with just one sheet of information for each customer. You may be able to just use a current form and add a few numbers to it.
   C. For setting up the recurring entries, you will need to compile a list of customer numbers, customer names, amounts, and perhaps frequency.
   D. For setting up the terms codes and the product codes (if applicable), you will need to compile appropriate lists of those codes.

V. Data entry and verification
   A. Use the above worksheets to enter the amounts.
   B. Print out the appropriate reports and verify the amounts against the original worksheets.
   C. Make corrections as necessary.

FIGURE 4.2 Accounts Receivable Conversion Checklist (con.)

VI. Operator training (for day-to-day operations)
  A. Formal training
    1. Send employees to classes.
    2. Training sessions with specialist (who knows that accounting software and is familiar with your accounting system)
  B. Informal training
    1. Tutorials
    2. On-the-job training (from someone in the company who has been trained)
    3. Discussion groups (to answer questions, allay fears, describe benefits)

VII. System startup and testing
  A. Start entering transactions in parallel to your current system.
    1. Note that your live invoices and statements should be coming from your manual system and that you should be printing facsimiles on plain white paper (if applicable to your software).
  B. At the completion of the first accounting period (usually a month), print the invoice register, the journal entry listings, the customer ledger, and other reports, and compare them to the manual system.
  C. Locate the source of any discrepancies and make adjustments.

VIII. Integration of modules
  A. Be sure that each additional module is running correctly in a stand-alone mode before integrating it into the rest of your system.
  B. Use an extra (duplicate diskette) copy of your accounting data (for the modules involved) to do a trial integration (i.e., do a parallel run to your computer system).
  C. Print out the appropriate reports and check the integration results.
  D. Locate the source of any problems, make adjustments, and try it again.
  E. Only when it is working correctly should you integrate your live system.

IX. Final documentation of your micro-accounting procedures
  A. As you start up your daily entry on the computer system, make notes as to how that entry is being performed. (step by step, in detail, plus notes on common or anticipated errors and how to recover from them).
  B. Compile the notes on the various operations into an organized document.
  C. Test the document by carrying out every step listed.

FIGURE 4.3 Accounts Payable Conversion Checklist

I. Study current system.
   A. See Section 2.3, "Accounting Needs."

II. Design new system.
   A. Determine what, if any, recurring entries will be needed.
   B. Design vendor number.
   C. Determine what information is to be accumulated on each vendor.
   D. Design format of checks, if applicable to your software.
   E. Order checks to fit the new system.
   F. Determine password system.

III. Set up software structure (differs significantly between brands of software).
   A. Enter the new user information, such as company name and address, passwords, and, sometimes, type of printer, balance forward date, and so on.
   B. Enter the desired report formats (if applicable).
   C. Verify all of the data that has been entered, by printing out and proofing the appropriate reports.
   D. Make corrections as necessary.

IV. Gather and organize data.
   A. Determine the input form for setting up the payables (what specific information, and the order in which it will be needed).
   B. Locate the data items and determine how much gathering and compiling will be needed. You want to end up with just one sheet of information for each vendor. You may be able to just use a current form and add a few numbers to it.
   C. For setting up the recurring entries, you will need to compile a list of vendor numbers, names, amounts, and, perhaps, frequency.
   D. For setting up the terms codes, you will need to compile an appropriate list.

V. Data entry and verification
   A. Use the above worksheets to enter the amounts.
   B. Print out the appropriate reports and verify the amounts against the original worksheets.
   C. Make corrections as necessary.

VI. Operator training (for day-to-day operations)
   A. Formal training
      1. Send employees to classes.
      2. Training sessions with specialist (who knows that accounting software and is familiar with your accounting system)

- B. Informal training
    1. Tutorials
    2. On-the-job training (from someone in the company who has been trained)
    3. Discussion groups (to answer questions, allay fears, describe benefits)

VII. System testing and startup
- A. Start entering transactions, in parallel to your current system.
    1. Note that your live checks should be coming from your manual system and that you should be printing facsimiles on plain white paper.
- B. At the completion of the first accounting period (usually a month), print the check register, the journal entry listings, the vendor ledger, and other reports, and compare them to the manual system.
- C. Locate the source of any discrepancies and make adjustments.

VIII. Integration of modules
- A. Be sure that each additional module is running correctly in a stand-alone mode before integrating it into the rest of your system.
- B. Use an extra (duplicate diskette) copy of your accounting data (for the modules involved) to do a trial integration (i.e., do a parallel run to your computer system).
- C. Print out the appropriate reports and check the integration results.
- D. Locate the source of any problems, make adjustments, and try again.
- E. Only when it is working correctly should you integrate your live system.

IX. Final documentation of your micro-accounting procedures
- A. As you start up your daily entry on the computer system, make notes as to how that entry is being performed (step by step, in detail, plus notes on common or anticipated errors and how to recover from them).
- B. Compile the notes on the various operations into an organized document.
- C. Test the document by carrying out every step listed.

FIGURE 4.3 Accounts Payable Conversion Checklist (con.)

I. Study current system.
   A. See Section 2.3, "Accounting Needs."

II. Design new system.
   A. Design employee numbers.
   B. Determine what information is to be accumulated on each employee.
   C. Determine the various non-tax deductions needed for the various employees and label them as required by the software.
   D. Determine which non-tax deductions are automatic.
   E. Design format of checks, if applicable to your software.
   F. Order checks to fit the new system.
   G. Determine password system

III. Set up software structure (procedures differ significantly between brands of software).
   A. Enter the new user information, such as company name and address, passwords, and, sometimes, type of printer, balance forward date, and so on.
   B. Enter the desired report formats (if applicable).
   C. Verify all of the data that has been entered by printing out and proofing the appropriate reports.
   D. Make corrections as necessary.

IV. Gather and organize data.
   A. Determine the input form for setting up the employees (what specific information and the order in which it will be needed).
   B. Locate the data items and determine how much gathering and compiling will be needed. You want to end up with just one sheet of information for each employee. You may be able to just use a current form and add a few numbers to it.
   C. Compile the input forms.
   D. For setting up the tax tables (if not supplied within the software), you will need to compile a list of tables needed and gather together copies of those tables (as in the "Employer's Tax Guide," Circular E, from the Internal Revenue Service).

V. Data entry and verification
   A. Use the above worksheets and tax tables to enter the amounts.
   B. Print out the appropriate reports and verify the amounts against the original worksheets.
   C. Make corrections as necessary.

FIGURE 4.4 Payroll Conversion Checklist

VI. Operator training (for day-to-day operations)
   A. Formal training
      1. Send employees to classes.
      2. Training sessions with specialist (who knows that accounting software and is familiar with your accounting system)
   B. Informal training
      1. Tutorials
      2. On-the-job training (from someone in the company who has been trained)
      3. Discussion groups (to answer questions, allay fears, describe benefits)

VII. System testing and startup
   A. Start entering transactions, in parallel to your current system.
      1. Note that your live payroll checks should be coming from your manual system and that you should be printing facsimiles on plain white paper.
   B. At the completion of the first payroll, print the payroll check register, the journal entry listings, the employee ledger, and other reports, and compare them to the manual system.
   C. Locate the source of any discrepancies and make adjustments.

VIII. Integration of modules
   A. Be sure that each additional module is running correctly in a stand-alone mode before integrating it into the rest of your system.
   B. Use an extra (duplicate diskette) copy of your accounting data (for the modules involved) to do a trial integration (i.e., do a parallel run to your computer system).
   C. Print out the appropriate reports and check the integration results.
   D. Locate the source of any problems, make adjustments, and try again.
   E. Only when it is working correctly should you integrate your live system.

IX. Final documentation of your micro-accounting procedures
   A. As you start up your daily entry on the computer system, make notes as to how that entry is being performed (step by step, in detail, plus notes on common or anticipated errors and how to recover from them).
   B. Compile the notes on the various operations into an organized document.
   C. Test the document by carrying out every step listed.

FIGURE 4.4 Payroll Conversion Checklist (con.)

5

STANDARD OPERATING PROCEDURES

5.1 THE SYSTEM MANAGER

Every company with a computer system should assign one employee to be the system manager, to oversee the operation of the system. This includes overseeing the equipment needs and maintenance, the use of proper operating procedures, and any security control systems in effect. This does not mean that you need to hire a computer expert. It means that you must have at least one person who is familiar with your equipment and software, and with the procedures for using it.

The person who originally shopped for the system and dealt with the consultants and/or salespeople, usually ends up as the system manager (either officially or unofficially). Everyone naturally turns to this person with their questions and problems because he or she has learned so much about the system during the acquisition process. In a small business, this is often one of the owners, and so it should be. It is difficult to delegate either the acquisition or the operational responsibilities of such a significant part of your business.

The use of the system must be monitored and

controlled, or the efficiency will fall drastically. The more people who are using the system, the more the operations must be structured. The following example illustrates this point.

If you are the only person who uses a certain printer, then you will not usually run into any surprises. Every time you go to use that printer, it will be set up as you left it, and you will have no difficulty in using it. If that printer is also used by several other people and there are no procedures set up concerning its use, problems arise quickly. You never know what state you are going to find the printer in. Each time you go to use it, you have to check all of the various options on the printer, such as the typeface, the type of ribbon loaded, the type of paper loaded, the number of lines per page, and many others. What actually happens in this situation is that you will check the major items, then try to use the printer. If the printer works as expected, fine; if it doesn't, then you must make adjustments and try it again. This is both frustrating and inefficient.

Each piece of computer equipment has certain rules for proper use that maximize the life of the equipment or ensure that the computer programs run as designed. The system manager will have to learn the rules appropriate for your equipment configuration by studying the equipment manuals, taking classes, and/or training with a consultant. The operators can then be trained in turn by the system manager. When questions or problems arise that the system manager cannot answer, he or she will be the one to contact the consultants or the computer dealer.

If your firm is growing, your computer system will surely be expanding as you make use of additional facets of the computer's power. Your system manager should be involved in any decisions to make changes or additions. This will ensure that the needs seen at the operational level are presented and that compatibility issues are considered.

When the computer system is first installed, appropriate operating procedures should be set up that will be able to handle both your current situation and your projected growth for the next few years. The dealer who sells you the equipment will sometimes aid in this project. If a consulting firm helps with your system conversion, they will probably recommend procedures consistent with the training they provide and document them for you.

We emphasize these operating procedures and their documentation for two reasons. First, everyone involved has to learn so much: a new type of equipment, new forms, new reports, new activities, and, sometimes, new ways of interacting with customers and vendors. Second, the computer requires precision in its use; each command and operation must be done just so, if the result is to be as desired. Only by organizing the procedures and writing them down will you achieve consistent results. The computer equipment and software manuals were written to cover every possible situation, so you will find them inappropriate as procedures manuals for your particular situation.

The system manager will also oversee any security controls you set up for the system. This might include one or more levels of password systems, controlling the distribution and use of diskettes, and monitoring the backup system.

A system's passwords, and any programs used to establish or change them, should be stored in a safe place. A safe-deposit box is ideal. The passwords should be changed whenever an operator leaves or if there is other reason to believe that confidentiality has been lost. Even if you do not wish to use passwords for security reasons, it is a good idea to assign an easy code to certain operations to prevent their accidental startup. Typing the wrong key at certain menu screens can get you started on an undesired operation, and attempts to escape from such a sequence can be disastrous as well as frustrating.

5.2 SCHEDULING THE COMPUTER AND DISKETTES

Many small companies that buy a single-user PC plan to use it for several different applications rather than limit its use to accounting. A multi-user microcomputer may be more than the company wants to deal with for a first computer. A PC is less of a commitment, in both time and money, so it is easier to decide to buy one.

If you plan to use a single-user PC for other applications besides accounting, the access to the computer will have to be controlled. Not only do you have to consider the security of the accounting data, but you may also run into conflicts about the availability of the machine. The easiest way to prevent such conflicts is to schedule computer use. For example, you might assign Monday, Tuesday, and Wednesday as days when the computer is exclusively for accounting, Thursday for management (analysis and projections), and the rest of the time the computer could be available on a sign-up basis.

Also consider the location of the computer. The easiest way to share a PC between departments is to put it into its own room, so that its use does not require bothering one person or one department all of the time. The key to that room can then be signed in and out. In some situations a roll-around cart can work out well. It depends on the distances involved, the number of cables that must be detached each time, and the frequency of the moves. Can the printer be on the same cart, or will it remain in one location?

If you have another heavy use, such as word processing, you may find that scheduling does not resolve the conflict. If both uses have been implemented successfully, the conflict probably indicates that a second PC is justified.

If you are sharing a floppy based system, the accounting data is easier to secure. Since it is stored on floppy diskettes, it can be locked up in the accounting department while the PC is doing other chores. The other departments will have their own set of program diskettes and sensitive data. In this situation, the system manager would probably want to set up a diskette library system and assign one person to act as librarian.

The library can be as simple as a lockable diskette box and a sign-out log. Such diskette holders are sold by most office supply stores. They store 50 or 80 diskettes vertically, separated by labeled tabs. The librarian signs out program diskettes, data diskettes, and backup diskettes appropriate to the task at hand and properly stores them when they are returned. Each diskette can always be located, and the chance of accidental or intentional abuse is lessened.

For this to work, the librarian must be given responsibility for all of the department's program diskettes, data diskettes, and new blank diskettes. As new diskettes are purchased, the librarian can label each one with a unique number before they are distributed and used.

The sharing of a hard disk PC system is the least secure situation for your accounting data. Many hard disk systems offer no password security for their contents. Anyone using the computer can alter, erase, or take copies of any files stored on the hard disk. Even if special procedures or special diskettes are needed to start up the computer, the stored data is still vulnerable whenever the PC has been left turned on. Frequently used PCs are usually left on during the working day, so the turn-on procedures and delays can be avoided.

If a hard disk PC is used by a single department, then there is some control over the use. It would be fairly noticeable whenever someone from outside that department came in and started using the computer, and the office containing it could be locked at closing time. But when a PC is shared more widely, control is lost. As a result, several companies now offer products that will add password systems to the more popular hard disks, such as the IBM XT. There are also products that will encrypt the data as it is stored, but for most businesses this is not desirable (it slows down computer operations drastically).

5.3 DATA ENTRY SESSIONS

Data Entry

Once your accounting system has been set up, most of your use of it will be inputting data and retrieving reports. Data entry should be organized into sessions rather than carried out haphazardly. The major source of errors in a computerized accounting system is the entry of incorrect data. Use of data entry sessions will decrease the number of input errors and will also allow you to find and correct such errors more easily.

Data entry is most efficient and accurate when the operator can concentrate on that task for a few hours without interruptions or distractions. You might need to have daily entry sessions and weekly report production, or you might be able to get away with two entry sessions and one reporting session each month. It depends on the volume of your business and on how precisely up-to-date you want to keep your accounting system.

A typical data entry session consists of several parts. These might include all or a portion of the following: data accumulation and preparation, data input, data verification, data file backup, posting to the journals, and printing transaction listings. First, you may want to accumulate data until there is enough for a couple of hours' work on the computer. For a small company, this might mean just two data entry sessions per month for accounts payable, for example. Then the data is prepared, or put into a form that will be straightforward to enter, to avoid constantly shuffling and searching through the original documents at the computer console.

When the data is ready to be entered, the operator signs onto the accounting system, going through the procedures that have been set up to control the system's use. The operator then enters the accumulated data, using the editing features that are built into the program being used.

Since no one can continuously enter large amounts of data perfectly, it is important that these accounting systems be designed to catch entry errors as they happen and to make it easy to correct them. Most programs check that only numbers are entered for amounts and that only valid account numbers are used. Other ways to catch entry errors are to use a batch entry system and to use the fact that every transaction entry has two sides that should be equal.

Batching the Data

Because of the importance of getting the data into the system correctly, some PC accounting systems use batch systems for data entry. This means that the financial transactions are not just typed into the computer in any order or in short spurts. They must be divided into batches and prepared for entry before being typed in. Each batch is assigned a unique number and tracked through the system as an entity. For each batch, the computer can easily accumulate totals on any or all of the numbers that are entered, including account numbers and reference numbers as well as dollar amounts. If these same numbers are totaled manually before they are entered into the computer, the totals can be compared to the computer's totals. They will seldom match unless all of the numbers have been typed in correctly.

The Solomon III accounting system uses a batch system. When the operator selects Data Entry—Journal Transactions, the first thing the system does is to assign a new and unique batch number and ask for the batch control amount. The batch control amount means that the system expects the operator to have previously added up the amounts of all of the transactions in that batch. That sum is used by the computer to compare with its own summation. Note that the debit amounts must be summed separately from the credit amounts; otherwise, the sum would normally be zero. Note also that Solomon III does not accumulate batch totals on any numbers except transaction amounts.

After a batch of transactions has been entered, Solomon III displays the totals and gives the operator a choice among making changes, deleting the whole batch, storing the batch, or posting the batch.

MBSI and CYMA accounting systems are less structured. CYMA has you select the journal you want to work in, then it continuously displays four totals: the Document Total, the Batch Total, the Journal Total, and the Ledger Total. The Document Total starts at zero each time a new source document number is entered. If one invoice has several journal entries to different accounts, the Document

Total should match the total on that invoice when all of its line items have been entered. The Batch Total is the accumulation of all entry amounts entered into this journal at this session. It is reset to zero whenever that data entry screen is exited, including when you change to the same data entry screen for a different journal. The Journal Total is a running total of all entries that have been made to that particular journal. The Ledger Total is a balancing total of all entries and all balance forwards. It continuously shows the amount your ledger is out-of-balance, so it should always equal zero.

With CYMA, each batch is not given a unique number; instead, each individual transaction is assigned a unique number by the system. Posting is not done by batch. All of the unposted transactions are posted whenever you carry out the posting operation. You can use the Batch Total and the Journal Total to use CYMA as a batch system if you set up the procedures to do so (the debit entries must be entered as a separate batch from the credit entries).

MBSI displays the number of transactions that have been entered and the running balance (which should equal zero, if the credits entered equal the debits entered). Both of these numbers are zeroed whenever you carry out the posting operation.

Editing

The ease of editing the entries as they are entered into the computer affects the speed of data entry in several ways. If it is easy to correct typing mistakes as they happen, the operator can work faster when entering the data. If it is hard to correct such errors, then more effort will go into entering the numbers and letters perfectly, slowing down the process (just as with typing). Here is how some programs handle data entry and editing.

Both CYMA and MBSI have you enter each transaction as several line items of one display screen. To correct something on the same line that you are on, you can use the backspace key to erase what you have just typed, then type it over. In CYMA, if you notice an error on a previous line, you enter a letter "f" at the next line. This will move you back up the display to the previous line. To move back five lines, enter "f" five times. When the error is reached, the entry can be reentered correctly. In MBSI, to accomplish the same correction you first finish entering the rest of the data for that transaction. Then the program asks, FIELD NUMBER TO CHANGE? You type in the line number of the incorrect entry and are allowed to retype that item.

To go back later and make a change to a transaction in MBSI, you are asked for the account number involved. The first transaction entered (since the last posting operation) will appear on the display. You can then step through all of the transactions for that account number, one at a time, using a single key. When you get to the transaction you are looking for, you can make the changes desired.

In CYMA, if you know the Entry Number that was assigned to the transaction you are looking for, you type it in to recall the transaction. If you don't know the Entry Number, you can call to the display a report listing all of the transactions by entry sequence, by Document Number, or by Transaction Date, and find the Entry Number you need.

Solomon III has designed its input screens so that each transaction is on a single line. There are columns for each item to be entered: account number, reference number, date, description, debit amount, and credit amount. As you enter each item, the program automatically shifts over to the next column. You can enter 13 transactions before the screen is filled, and you can just keep entering more after that. What happens is that as each new transaction is added, the top one disappears from the display, so the screen continues to show 13 transactions. The computer continues to store all of the information you have entered, even though you can no longer see it.

If you want to see a transaction that is not already displayed, the program will *scroll* the transactions up or down at your command. If you tell it to scroll down, the earlier transactions will appear one at a time at the top of the display, and the most recent ones will be pushed off at the bottom of the display. If you tell it to scroll up, transactions appear at the bottom and disappear at the top of the display; when the last transaction entered appears, the scrolling stops. You can also go directly to the top or the bottom of the list, or you can insert or delete transactions, with the push of a single key. When the display is not scrolling, you can use the four directional ARROW keys on the keyboard to move the *cursor* (screen pointer) over to any item on the screen that you want to change. When you are finished working on that particular batch of transactions, you push the ESCAPE key to exit that operation.

One advantage of Solomon's approach is that it is easy for a new user to visualize what is occurring. In this case, each batch of transactions appears as if it is organized and stored as a long list of transactions, of which only a portion can be viewed at any one time. This clear and familiar analogy is easy to learn and use.

Verifying

As financial transactions are entered into the accounting system, they are usually first stored in some temporary area, to allow you to make any additions, changes, or deletions needed. The computer system will offer or force a report listing of the transactions just entered. Use this listing to check the transactions entered; if possible, have someone other than the person who entered them do the checking.

Posting

When you judge the transactions to be in good order, you instruct the accounting system to post them. This means that the transaction amounts are added to the appropriate accounts, including general ledger accounts, customer accounts, vendor accounts, employee accounts, and so on. Once this has been done, further direct changes are usually not allowed. Instead, any changes must be made by *adjusting journal entries.*

This is because the posting operation is considered to be when the information actually becomes a part of your permanent accounting records. You want to prevent any changes to your permanent records that do not leave an audit trail; otherwise, anyone could go into your records and make changes without your knowledge. Even if you want to go in and make some changes yourself, a trail will ensure that a year later you will be able to see what occurred, and you will not have amounts appear or disappear mysteriously.

Generally, the posting operation should be done at the end of each data entry session, after the entries have been listed and verified. With some systems, posting is automatic at this time; with others, the data will not be posted until someone commands the program to do so. If there are unresolved questions and the posting is delayed, your records will not be current. Any management reports printed may have some serious omissions. Posting can take quite a while, depending on how many transactions you have saved up and on how fast your computer system is. If your system has a large number of transactions running through it, daily posting will lessen the delays at the end of the month.

Many accounting systems refuse to post a set of transactions if they are not in balance. The reasoning is that to do so will just aggravate the problem. If such a set of transactions are posted, then the whole general ledger will be out-of-balance. It is much easier to locate and correct such a problem in a small set of transactions than in the full ledger.

In Solomon III you must select whether to store or post each batch when you are finished entering transactions. You can store any batch for later editing; you don't have to post it when you first enter it. When you are ready to post a batch, you release it for posting. The actual posting process is a separate operation. When you instruct the system to Post Transactions, all of the batches that have been released for posting will be posted. In addition to the Post Transactions command, every time you sign off of the system, Solomon III asks you if you want to post transactions. This is a handy way to accomplish the same thing routinely. Solomon III refuses to post if a transaction batch is not in balance.

CYMA and MBSI each have a command for posting to the general ledger. That command simply posts all unposted transactions that have been entered since the last posting command. Both brands will post a set of transactions that is out-of-balance (There is no reason for allowing such out-of-balance posting).

After the data entry, verification, and posting, the operator should always make backup copies of the new data. This is so important that it has a section of its own—Section 5.4.

The only exception to this is if there are several short sessions on the same day; in that case, a backup operation at the end of the day would be sufficient. The most that could then be lost would be one day's worth of data input.

5.4 BACKUPS AND RECOVERIES

The most valuable part of your computerized accounting system will be the records of your company that are accumulated over time. The hardware and the programs can be repaired or replaced, but your data can be lost forever. To protect yourself against such loss, you must back up your data on a regular basis. To back up your data means to make duplicate copies of it, so that if anything happens to the copy being used, you can recover your system. You will actually want to have several copies, with at least one stored off-site (a safe-deposit box is good for this).

There are many situations that a proper backup system will save you from: the fragility of floppy diskettes and hard disks; procedural mistakes; fluctuations in the electrical lines; and even intentional sabotage or tampering.

Floppy diskettes are reliable if they are properly cared for, but even with the best of care something unforeseen is sure to happen sooner or later. To minimize the possibility, always handle the diskettes carefully. Keep them in their covers unless they are in the computer. Keep them in their storage box if they are not in the computer. Diskettes lying around on the desk top or in the desk drawers are a sure sign of a disaster waiting to happen.

But with a good backup system, you won't have to worry about what might happen. A good backup system is one that you know works because you test it occasionally, one that you understand and feel comfortable with. The question why to back up is easy to explain. The when to back up, what to back up, and how to back up questions are more difficult. They depend on your transaction volumes, what accounting system you use, and what type of hardware you use.

There are two types of backup: backup done for archival purposes and backup done in case the working data is destroyed, damaged, or suspected to be incorrect for any reason. The archival copies are usually made at the end of every month, so that at the end of each year you have 12 diskettes that together contain the detailed information for the whole year. The same information is stored in the reports that are printed out at the end of each month, so those diskettes are not necessary for your archives. Having the diskettes allows you to run other reports later and may be handier to use for reference if your paper records are stored deep in some storeroom or at a remote location.

The major reason for making backups is for protecting your investment. However, the data you are protecting is continually changing, so a duplicate copy is not protection for very long. Another consideration is how many duplicates to make, since a single one may not be enough protection. Over the years the data processing industry has learned some effective ways to protect such dynamic information.

The key to these procedures is to use a rotational scheme, such as having one backup diskette for each day of the week or using a grandparent-parent-child rotation. The day-of-the-week procedure copies the data onto one backup diskette on Monday, then that diskette is stored. The following Monday that same diskette is used to copy the data again. (In the process the data stored on that diskette a week earlier gets erased to make room for the new data.) A second diskette is used for Tuesdays, a third for Wednesdays, and so on.

This is a good procedure as long as the system is updated and backed up several days of every week. If data entry is only done on Mondays, for example, then only the Monday backup diskette has any value, and you no longer have a multilevel backup system. The Monday diskette is your only copy, and if anything happens during the backup operation, you may suddenly have no workable copies.

The grandparent-parent-child procedure is more general in purpose. It is a three-diskette rotation that always uses the oldest copy for the next backup operation. If you are the only one using this system, then you can physically implement it. After setting up three backup diskettes in a standard storage area, always use the one at the top of the stack, then replace it at the bottom of the stack. Whether it has been three weeks or three hours since your last backup operation, you will always use the oldest copy, keeping the two more recent copies in reserve.

For a more formal implementation of this cycle, label the three backup diskettes as A, B, and C and keep a backup log. Each time the operators carry out a backup operation, have them make an entry into the backup log. The entry must include the operator's initials, the date and time, the diskette used, and a comment on what changes were made to the data during that entry session. This way you will always be able to tell exactly what is on each one of your backup copies.

And now we come to some real nitty-gritty details of backing up. Does each different module get its own set of backup diskettes? Do the different modules each have their own rotation, or do they all get backed up every time? When is it necessary to back up onto tape cassettes instead of onto floppy diskettes? These are all matters of diskette capacity, of data security, and of the way the various modules interact.

There is no single correct answer, of course. In the past, most systems were either floppy diskette based or had large hard disks with built-in tape cassettes for backup. Both of these situations have easy answers. The floppy system should just make duplicates of each data diskette that has been used since the last backup session; there should be a set of three backup diskettes for each data diskette. The hard disk system would usually copy the entire contents of the hard disk onto one tape cassette; that is easier than trying to be selective.

Today many PCs are purchased that have hard disks, but no tape cassette drive. The solution here is to back up the important data onto floppy diskettes. The problem is diskette capacity. It takes dozens of diskettes to hold all of the data that fits on a hard disk. In order to minimize the time spent on backup operations, you want to copy only those files that have been changed since the last backup. There are many ways to accomplish this, but all of them are best implemented by someone who is familiar with both the operating system and the accounting system involved.

Here are some of the problems you may run into. Let's say you back up your accounts payable data after sessions on that module and the payroll data after payroll sessions. You might have several accounts payable sessions before you need to have a payroll session. If you use just one set of backup diskettes for both of those modules, it would be difficult to determine which diskette to use at the end of each session. In fact, if there were three accounts payable sessions between payroll sessions, the three backup diskettes would be rotated so that the payroll data would be copied onto the same diskette both times. Instead of having a three-diskette rotation, you would have a single payroll backup diskette.

Actually, only the smallest companies could possibly fit the monthly data from two or more modules onto a single diskette. A system with a hard disk is likely to be used to accumulate detailed transaction data for a whole year; as a result, the data files will grow extremely large. Later in the year it will probably take several diskettes to hold one copy of that data each time it is backed up. Eventually, it is necessary to buy a tape cassette drive rather than continue to struggle with increasing numbers of diskettes.

Another consideration for backing up is the interaction among the various modules. If you enter some receipts of goods into your purchase order module, for example, the system will usually update your inventory (quantity on hand) files and perhaps your job cost files as well. With a floppy system this is obvious, because the system asks you to insert the various data diskettes as it requires them. But on a hard disk system, the system always has access to all of the data files, and you cannot tell which ones it is changing. You may just back up your purchase order data files, not realizing that you must also back up your inventory and job cost files. The rule is that if the modules interact any way, they must be backed up as a unit in order to maintain their interrelationships.

On the other hand, many systems have modules that interact with the general ledger module, but only when told to by the operator. In such cases, the modules can be backed up separately, saving significant amounts of time. Remember, anything that will make the backup operation easier or faster will not only save you money every day, but it will also increase the chances of the backup operation being done regularly and correctly.

Recovering

Whenever something happens that forces you to rely on your backup data, you must go through another procedure, called *recovery*. This procedure is performed so seldom that the chance of errors is great, yet it is very important to be able to recover as much of your data as possible. That is why you keep three levels of backup data instead of just one; it gives you three chances to achieve a successful recovery. It is also important to test your recovery procedure when you first set up your system, or you will not know whether it works until it is too late.

Any recovery procedure should include certain steps. We will first list three steps in summary form, then discuss them briefly.

1. Determine the cause of the problem.
2. Correct the problem.
3. Test the microcomputer system.
4. Write-protect the backup diskette(s) involved.
5. Make a duplicate copy of the most recent backup diskette(s).
6. Replace the incorrect or suspected data.
7. Test the accounting system.

You must determine the cause of the problem so that your backup diskettes will not inadvertently become victims of the same problem. Often it is clear what happened. Perhaps the period closing was done incorrectly and needs to be redone, or there was a power outage that scrambled the data. At other times there is no indication how the reports suddenly became scrambled or why the program started throwing error messages onto the display.

If the problem is apparent, then you can usually take corrective and/or preventative steps. Often the problem is not easily determined but seems to have gone away. If diagnostic tests of the system can find no faults, you may have to risk one of your backup copies to see how the accounting system is working. But don't just insert the backup diskette into the computer. Since you only want to read the data from the backup diskettes at this time and not alter the data in any way, you should stick a write-protect tab over the write-protect notch on each backup diskette. This prevents any accidental alteration. A further precaution is to make a copy of the backup diskette before using it. If there is a second computer available, use it to make the copy.

Never use more than one of your backup copies until the problem has definitely been solved. Here is one common problem that illustrates why. A contaminant (peanut butter, for example) somehow gets onto the surface of a working diskette. This will naturally interfere with the computer's ability to retrieve information from that diskette, and the cause of the problem may not be apparent. More importantly, some of the peanut butter will be transferred onto the diskette drive's reading mechanism, which will in turn contaminate any diskette subsequently used. You can see how easily all three of your backup copies could be contaminated if the recovery procedure were not controlled.

The actual technique of replacing the data files with backup data depends on the operating system and the accounting system involved. The process should be aided by someone familiar with both systems. The testing of the accounting system would usually consist of trying the questionable operations and printing out the applicable reports.

5.5 REPORTS AND INQUIRIES

As with any computer system, micro-accounting systems can provide many different reports, all crammed with data. But what you want is quality rather than quantity, so you must be selective about which reports to print out and how often. You also want to minimize the duplication of effort that can occur if everyone prints out reports according to their own needs without coordinating with the report needs of others. You can accomplish both of these by organizing the report printing.

This means setting up a schedule. Each report should be named and described, with production dates and a list of the regular recipients. Then everyone knows when to expect different reports, and they know what reports are available. This cannot be a rigid schedule; too many exceptions occur. People occasionally require a report ahead of its scheduled date, and they often request additional reports that are not distributed to them on a regular basis.

This organization will also help you control access to reports containing sensitive information. Each report can have a list of authorized recipients associated with it, so the computer operators (or diskette librarians) know when they are receiving authorized requests.

To develop such a schedule, you will have to determine both the demand and the production costs involved for each report. The demand is who needs which reports and how often. Production costs are important because some accounting reports are only available after significant effort is made by your accounting staff, and because some reports tie up the computer for hours while they are being printed.

Start by listing every report available from the system, by title and description. It is helpful to organize this list, first by the accounting modules that are in your system, and then by the following four types of reports provided by these systems. Management reports include the standard financial statements, various analyses, and aging reports. There are interactive inquiries, where the computer operator calls up specific items of information from within the system, such as information about a single customer or a single order. Working reports include such things as purchase orders, sales orders, ledgers, and the trial balance worksheet. Then there are the audit trail reports, which are listings of transactions entered (journal entries), and of changes or deletions to customer files, vendor files, general ledger accounts, and so forth.

Distribute the list of reports and ask your staff members to note which reports they need to see and how often. Find out which of the reports can be circulated and which will have to have a separate copy for each recipient. (For these, the copy machine will be far more effective than printing multiple copies with the computer.) Of course, some people will ask for an update of their reports every morning, but you should get them to start with their minimum requirements.

Next, try to determine the effort and computer time involved in the production of the reports. Your accounting staff should be able to say which reports will require accounting efforts, such as bringing the books up to date and adding the proper adjusting entries before accurate financial statements can be generated. Your consultant or software dealer can tell you which reports will require long printing operations. These generally involve those areas where you have the most activity. If you have many items in inventory, then your inventory status and analysis reports will tie up the computer.

The reason some of the report printing is so slow is because the reports are lengthy and involve a lot of sorting and computations as the data to be printed is selected and compiled from the vast store of data in the system. In word processing the bottleneck is often the printer, and in that case a faster printer and/or a print buffer will solve the problem. In accounting, the bottleneck is the program itself, not the printer. Often a slow printer will perform as well as a fast one, because both must frequently wait for the accounting program to spit out a few more numbers or letters.

You should now have a general idea of your printing needs and when they occur. Usually the end-of-the-month processing is when the worst crunch happens. That is the time the system is being heavily used to close the accounting period and print the monthly statements and management reports. At the same time many reports have to be printed for the archival records before the transaction detail is erased to make room for next month's. Unless your business is very small, you will probably have to make some adjustments to your first printing schedule because of this cycle.

Another consideration in report printing is the paper and forms to be used. For an extensive conversion involving several modules, the computer might be expected to print out checks, sales orders, purchase orders, invoices, customer statements, and accounting reports on white paper 14 inches across. Each of these forms is readily available from computer supply houses as blank forms, serially numbered, and attached together into one long continuous sheet. One end is fed into the printer and aligned. From then on the sheets automatically advance one at a time as required by the accounting program.

With just a single printer, you can see that these different continuous forms will have to be exchanged in the printer each time you need to print out something different. If you can group your operations into batches, this switching is minimized. However, if you want to print out sales orders as the orders are placed, invoices as the product is shipped, and checks at odd times throughout the day, then you will be switching the paper and forms in the printer continually.

5.6 END-OF-PERIOD PROCESSING (CLOSING)

In a manual system, the books are closed at the end of each monthly accounting period, and then the reports are prepared. It is usually several weeks or longer before the reports are finally ready. This closing consists of posting the various journals to the ledger, running a trial balance worksheet, then making the appropriate standard and adjusting entries. Although the same accounting operations are performed on a computerized system at the end of each month, there are several additional operations that must be performed. Nevertheless, it is much easier to close a period on a micro-accounting system than on a manual accounting system.

The steps to go through on a computerized system are as follows:

1. Make a backup copy of the accounting data.
2. Post the various journals to the ledger.
3. Print a trial balance worksheet.
4. Make appropriate standard, adjusting, and reversing journal entries, and post them.
5. Print and review the reports.
6. Repeat steps 3, 4, and 5 until the books are correct.
7. Make a backup copy of the data.
8. Print the final reports.
9. Make an archival copy of the data.
10. Tell the system to *update* the books.
11. Print any reports necessary to verify that the updating has been successfully completed.

The various backup copies are made in case anything goes wrong during the posting between modules or the updating of the accounts. If there are problems, it is then easy to make a copy of the backup data to start again. The update operation tells the computer system to purge from the records all of the detailed transaction information and to bring forward only the summary balance figure for each account. This is done to make room in the system for the new period's detailed information. After this is done, your only records of that detailed information are on your archival diskette and in your printed reports.

With a hard disk in the system, storage space is much less of a problem, and it is possible to keep a whole year's detailed information. To do so, the hard disk must be large enough to hold it, and the accounting system must offer that option. CYMA's general ledger has an especially nice way of handling this. Every time you tell it to print any report, it requests a range of dates to be covered. In August you can easily get a report covering January the first quarter, for example. To retain the detail, you just do not carry out the update operation. However, it is still a good idea to make an archival copy of the data each month.

Note that steps 3, 5, and 11 above require the printing of reports, perhaps several times. This is one place where it is handy to be able to print such reports to the display screen instead of to the printer. It is faster, quieter, and saves wear on the printer. CYMA allows all reports to be printed to the screen; most systems require all reports to go to the printer only.

Adjusting journal entries includes corrections, but it is more often used to handle such accounting items (non-cash transactions) as depreciation, deferred income, prepayments, and deposits on orders. For example, when equipment is received on which a deposit has been made, there will have to be an adjusting entry to transfer the deposit amount from the deposit account to the property and equipment account.

The term *closing* can be taken literally in a manual accounting system. When you close your books, you are saying that they are closed and locked as of that date. After that point no changes are to be made to them; any errors discovered later must be corrected by using adjusting entries that reverse the original (erroneous) entry and replace it with a correct one as of the current date. This is reasonable, considering all of the effort that went into preparing the reports after the closing. It also leaves a clear trail of what happened. If you went back to the correct date to make any changes, the reports would have to be prepared all over again so they would match the books. Also, there would be no indication of the error and correction.

A computer system can be more flexible than that, and many of the accounting systems take advantage of this and offer new ways of handling closings. For example, some allow you to post transactions to previous accounting periods even after they have been "closed." The reasoning is that the books will then reflect occurrences more accurately, as if everything had been accounted for correctly in the first place. You can then easily print out another set of financial reports that will reflect the corrected situation.

However, you will then have produced two sets of reports that are nearly identical, and it will often be very difficult to tell which set is which. Your staff and advisors could conceivably end up with many copies of several versions of reports, all with the same titles, headings, and so on.

Another feature some systems offer is the ability to enter transactions for the new accounting period, although the previous period has not yet been closed (updated). This allows time for the end-of-period accounting entries without forcing you to fall behind on the new period.

5.7 END-OF-YEAR PROCESSING

At the end of each fiscal year, you will first carry out the same operations as at the end of every monthly accounting period: the adjustments, the posting, the reports, the backups, and the updating. You will then instruct the accounting system to carry out the end-of-the-year processing. That tells the computer to add the past year's net profit or loss to the equity account and to zero all income and expense accounts. If you are running your system with previous-year comparative statements, the system will also update the month-end balances stored for each account so that the comparatives will reflect the year just ended.

This is also the time to set new budget figures into the system, if you are using that option. CYMA will automatically put the past year's monthly amounts for each account into the coming year's budgets, if you tell it to.

Many accounting systems refuse to allow you to delete an account that has had any activity in it; the account must remain in the system until the end of the year. (This is required by good accounting practices.) So this is the time to clear out those old accounts. After the computer has carried out the end-of-year processing, the system will allow you to delete them.

5.8 WHAT ABOUT YOUR ACCOUNTANTS AND CPA FIRM?

Before computerizing their books, many firms use outside accounting services and/or CPA firms. The accounting firm may look over the books and prepare financial statements and tax returns annually, or it may be deeply involved in the operations of the client's business. When a business converts its books onto an in-house computer, the relationship with such service firms can certainly change. Depending on the training and knowledge of your accounting staff, the PC can make you relatively independent of such services, or it may require the same periodic review and adjustments that your manual system required. At best, it will free up the accounting firm from the detail entry, giving it time to serve in an advisory role on more important matters.

Even though the computerized system will generate financial statements, you will still need the services of a CPA firm. You should have your accounting operations reviewed occasionally, to be sure that the entries into the computer system are being made correctly. Your banker, investors, and others will occasionally want to see financial statements that have been prepared by an independent CPA firm. You will still need tax planning and tax reporting services. If the inputs to your system are being made properly, all these accounting services can be accomplished more easily (and less expensively).

6

TRENDS IN MICRO-ACCOUNTING

Micro-accounting is currently fulfilling only a fraction of its potential usefulness, but it is advancing rapidly in capabilities, in sophistication, and in ease of use. This is mostly because the microcomputer hardware continues to increase in speed and capacity, which in turn allows software developers to design larger and more complex programs. For you, this means more features and/or more flexibility in your accounting systems. Here are some of the trends that are already happening.

6.1 MORE CAPABILITIES

On-line Help

Some of the newer packages offer explanations and reference material at the push of a key. This can be far superior to using the operator's manual, because it is handy, and it is already turned to the right page. Sometimes there are several levels of help; if that help screen doesn't answer your question, you can request further details on the subject.

Data Transfers Into Other Programs

Due to the extremely high demand for this capability, many vendors are announcing or offering ways to extract specified accounting data. Some are offering their own spreadsheet or database program that can use the data accumulated in their accounting modules. Others have developed a transfer module that lets you select what data you want, and then it puts it into a file that can be used by most of the popular spreadsheet, database, or word processing programs on the market.

If you are already using a spreadsheet, you would obviously prefer the second approach. Why should you have to buy and learn a new spreadsheet when you have already invested a lot of time and money in your old one. However, for companies buying their first system, it would be easier to learn just one vendor's line of products, since they are usually similar in operation.

Networks

Networks are also in high demand among small businesses. Networking allows you to connect your various microcomputers together so they can share hard disks, share that expensive printer, and grow into a multi-user system. The hardware for such networking is widely available, but there are many different versions. Each brand is completely different.

Because of this variation, the software vendors have a hard time converting their products to run on a network. Which network should they commit themselves to? A wrong choice can mean a big disadvantage later. So they tend to sit around and wait for IBM to introduce its network. That is always a safe choice, and when it does happen, many of the hardware vendors will also shift to that type of network. However, it has turned out to be a long wait.

Waiting also has this disadvantage: Those that make the right choice now will end up on the front seat of that bandwagon instead of running behind trying to jump on board. Several accounting software vendors have recently announced versions for networking, choosing from among the currently popular networks. Whatever happens, in a few years all of the major accounting systems will be available for some type of networking.

Remote Entry

Many small businesses do their accounting in one location, but have another location where business is done. A multiuser system would handle this, but that is much more expensive than a basic PC system. A limited but cost-effective solution for this is for the software to allow a remote stand-alone PC to accumulate transactions, and then later accept that data and merge it into the master data files in the accounting office. While there is no trend toward this, it is being developed by a couple of the vendors.

6.2 MORE SOPHISTICATION

This means that the programs are incorporating more of what you need, anticipating more of your questions, and providing you with more filtered and relevant information. A good example of this is the use of *exception reports*. This type of report doesn't force you to go through all of the data and pick out the items you are looking for; rather, the computer does that selection for you and prints out only the targeted items. If you wanted to know which of your vendors have been delivering a week late, you would prefer a simple list of them over a performance report that listed the delivery performance of every one of your vendors.

Other indications of increased sophistication are the handling of multiple companies, voided checks, batch processing, interrupted batch processes, integrated backup systems, and integrated audit trails that are transparent to the user.

Micro-accounting is developing in two directions. One

is toward more flexibility in the general accounting packages; the other is toward packages focused on specific industries. In the short run, the general packages will remain more popular because they currently provide a better solution to more users. In the long run, the focused packages will win out in almost every industry because they can meet specific needs better. But because each focused package necessarily addresses a much smaller market, they attract less attention and are subject to less developmental pressures (from accountants, for example). They will take longer to evolve into proven products.

6.3 SALES AND SUPPORT

Advances are also being made in this area. There is still a lot of experimentation in selling accounting software. No one knows the best way, or even a good way, to approach the 95 percent of businesses that have not yet computerized their accounting. Vendors are developing videotapes and diskettes that aid in product evaluation and training. Dealers are adding people with accounting backgrounds to their staffs or teaming up with local accounting firms to provide the extensive support needed for this type of software. Fewer dealers are telling customers they can provide adequate support for free.

6.4 SYNOPSIS

A few years down the road this all may become unimportant, as micro-accounting software continues to progress. In software, what appears to the user as a simple product may require extremely sophisticated and complex programming. An example of this is the operating system of the Apple MacIntosh computer. It is far easier to use than previous operating systems, yet it took thousands of hours to design and build. The Lotus 1-2-3/Symphony product is another example. The spreadsheet portion of that product is far more flexible and powerful than the original VisiCalc product, yet it is also easier to use. It could only achieve that by being a far more complex program.

We can expect accounting software to advance in that way, becoming more complex underneath, but appearing simple and easy to use. Today's most popular micro-accounting programs were originally designed for the old Apple II and CP/M-type micros, then translated to run on the newer machines. This means that those programs are still operating under design constraints from the older equipment. Other accounting programs have been converted from the large and expensive minicomputers. They have more features and accounting sophistication, but since they were developed several years ago, they tend to lack some of the recent innovations in software engineering (such as interactive help, inquiries to the display screen, and so on).

The newest developments in micro-accounting software are being made for the IBM-PC-type micros, and these programs are using the increased capacity to make the programs easier to use. And yet there is already a new generation of microcomputer hardware (called super-micros) that can accommodate even more complex programs. The software developers must feel that they will never catch up with the hardware.

There is a lot of room in today's hardware for more complex programs. The advances in software engineering will continue, and the newer software products will show more concern for the end-user and less concern for the constraints of the machinery. Micro-accounting today is still a do-it-yourself situation. Businesses that are waiting for a more friendly, packaged, ready-to-go solution to their problems will see it within a few years.

APPENDIX A
FOR PROFESSIONAL ACCOUNTANTS

A.1 WHY SHOULD YOU GET INVOLVED?

Professional accountants are just beginning to move into the field of microcomputer accounting. In the past computerized accounting was so expensive that only large accounting firms could deal with it, and they had specialized departments for that purpose. The advent of microcomputers and VisiCalc in 1976 started what is now a revolution in accounting for small businesses. But the early microcomputer systems required programming and computer expertise, and the early users were people who were willing to go out and learn those skills. Accounting firms were effectively excluded from all of the activity unless they also acquired these skills.

That is no longer the case. Today it is fairly easy to hook together the pieces of a microcomputer system, insert the packaged software, and start using the system. This is a boon for small businesses, and they are rapidly moving to computerize wherever they need it the most. A business's accountants should be its most valuable resource for that project, because they already know the current accounting system and the requirements of the situation.

Many accounting firms have avoided this area, feeling that it is going to take away much of their business. It is true that the more mundane aspects of write-up will be brought in-house by the client, but the need for independent verification and preparation of financial statements remains, along with the many other services CPAs provide and many new services created by the microcomputer. Think of it as a great opportunity. It is the only high-growth area of accounting, and there are many businesses out there that need your help with their conversions.

There are a number of ways you can help them. You evaluate the many programs available and advise shoppers on their relative merits. You can specialize in training in the use of one or more of the popular packages; both end-users and dealers would attend such classes. You can help businesses through the conversion process, as described in this book.

When your clients decide to bring in a microcomputer, are you going to be ready to help them, or are you going to watch as they go out and find another firm that *is* ready? In the following section we provide some ways for accounting firms to approach this new field of micro-accounting.

A.2 HOW TO GET STARTED IN MICRO-ACCOUNTING

Acquire a Microcomputer

The very first thing an accounting firm must do in entering this field is to acquire and use a microcomputer. This will not only allow you and your staff to learn to use a microcomputer system, it will force you to go through the same process you will be helping your clients go through. If you have a data processing staff, have them help, but also get the accounting staff involved. They are the ones who have to learn it so they will avoid surprises at clients' startups.

If you have no previous computer experience, start with a fairly basic system. Wait until later to go for advanced options such as hard disks, ramdisks, color, and graphics. The selection of a first printer is especially hard. An inexpensive dot matrix type is fine for training, but it may not be suitable for client correspondence and reports. You may need to hire a consultant or take some classes from your dealer.

Some other ways to learn about what is available in software are to join a *users' group*, join an organization like ITM, or to rent software. A users' group is just what it sounds like, and there are many of them across the country. The largest is the Boston Computer Society, which has over 10,000 members nationwide. Users' groups usually have subgroupings according to special interests. Accountants too are forming users' groups, within their own business communities, and at the state society level. ITM is a company that has accumulated information on almost all software on the market, and members can call up to make inquiries according to their needs. ITM also sells the software at a discount to members. We list ITM's address and phone number in the Software Bibliography. There are also newsletters directed specifically to accountants, such as the *CPA Computer Report* (Atlanta, Georgia, (404) 455-7600). And there are specialized magazines for accountants, like *Computers in Accounting* (New York, New York (212) 935-9210).

Renting software is somewhat controversial, because renters can easily make copies of the software and thus obtain it for free. Nevertheless, the common software is available for rent, by the week. See our discussion of software piracy in Chapter 3.

It is easiest to buy and learn a word processing program first, before you tackle spreadsheets or accounting packages. When you are ready for the accounting packages, you may want to buy one of the $400 all-in-one "bookkeeping" packages. That will show you how the low-end products work and give you some idea of what to look for in the high-end packages, which run from $3,000 to $5,000 for a full accounting program. (A little further on we will discuss specialized programs written just for accounting firms—the "client write-up" packages.

Learn to Use it Internally

Your second hurdle, after selecting and acquiring the system, is to integrate it into your business. If you just sit it somewhere and tell everyone, "There it is," very few people will use it. Usually there will be one or two people who will jump in and become quite expert, often spending their own time learning more about it. These are the people who take the manuals home each night to study them. The rest of your staff will avoid using the computer if left on their own.

You will need to plan how the PC will be used. How much is it to be used for your word processing chores and how much as a learning vehicle for your accounting staff? You will see right away that PCs do not lend themselves to being shared. Some people will become overly addicted to it, and others will use the unavailability as an excuse not to use it. Even you may have a change of heart about the training uses after you see how great it is for your word processing.

While every partner doesn't have to become an expert, it is important that they all support the microcomputer project. Also, someone in management must be assigned the responsibility of system manager. There will be numerous small decisions to be made, such as how to organize and store floppy diskettes, how often to make backup copies of data, and who will be doing which operations on the computer. The idea is to standardize these procedures so that everyone involved does them in the same way. You should also watch out for duplication of effort, such as two staff members designing similar tax planning spreadsheets.

It will be helpful for your firm to subscribe to one or two of the monthly magazines that specialize in the brand of computer you are using. These are the best ways to keep up to date on what is available for your system, and they always offer helpful hints on using the system. The store where you buy the system can tell you which are the good magazines for your machine.

Selecting Your Accounting Software

There is one major difference between your installation and that of other small businesses. You must select a system that will not only work for you, but will also help you work for your clients. This means considering compatibility and flexibility. The best situation is when you and your client use the same hardware and software. Then you can simply make a copy of your client's data onto a diskette and bring it back to use at your office. The popularity of IBM-type PCs means that such machine compatibility is not unusual. That leaves the software as the greater problem.

The software that best addresses your accounting

situation will often be entirely inappropriate for your clients. You have special billing needs, based on tracking the hours your staff spends on various projects; there are specialized Time & Billing programs available for CPA firms that fit that need. Similarly, there are special Client Write-up programs available. But they are high-priced and will not fit the needs of your clients that want to bring their accounting in-house.

You can handle this in any of three ways. The first way is to use a specialized program for a CPA firm but select a brand that also offers general-purpose accounting modules that will be appropriate for your small clients. Then you can set up your clients with the general modules they need, be compatible with their data, and still have the ability to carry out your specialized needs.

The second way to handle this issue is to use a good general accounting package for both your own firm and for your clients. The most significant feature you will miss will be the ability to do after-the-fact payroll for your write-up clients. Also, the Time & Billing package you use will not automatically integrate into your general ledger, so you will have to make summary journal entries for that purpose.

The third way to handle this is to use different brands of software for your internal accounting needs and for your clients' accounting needs. This is both unwieldy and expensive to support in your office, but it will happen occasionally. Usually it comes about because of the limitations in packaged software or because the client has already purchased the software.

A.3 PUTTING THE COMPUTER TO USE IN THE ACCOUNTING FIRM

As a CPA in public practice, it is important that you prepare yourself and your staff to meet the demand for computer assistance. For many of you this is already apparent in the requests that are coming in from your clients.

When it comes to microcomputers, accounting professionals come up against the same problems and perplexities as does everyone else. The advantages accountants have is a working knowledge of how the accounting process works. The logical steps are to (1) gain the necessary training needed to operate the computer and (2) learn how to operate and apply accounting software.

The CPA is faced with two hurdles when dealing with microcomputers. The first is computerizing the accounting firm. Typical applications are tax planning, preparation of audit schedules, client write-up, word processing, and other administrative applications. Once the CPA has tackled the internal applications, it is time to turn to client applications. After all, how can you teach someone a subject unless you first learn it yourself?

The accounting firm will have to go through the same processes as its clients. Selecting the software and hardware, installing it, training staff (professional staff and support staff), and, finally, using the computer and software in real situations.

Unfortunately, accountants—contrary to popular belief—don't have inherent insight into what computers and which software works in all possible situations. It is a learned skill, and even then you are still subject to your limitations and capacities as a human being. So you won't know all possible situations in which to apply software to either your own or your clients' needs. But you can concentrate on a few packages to get to know their secrets (the manuals don't cover *everything*) and then turn to helping your clients with their needs.

Once your computer(s) has been purchased, your software installed (usually a spreadsheet and a tax planning package at first), and the necessary training provided, you are ready to apply all of this to your daily work. Typically, the approach at this point is a short-term one. In the midst of all of the hoopla, the logistics of establishing a control system may be overlooked or delayed. After awhile chaos reigns—diskettes kept in drawers, workpaper files, briefcases in the coffee room (all without identifying labels, of course). Backup? What's that?

The issues of how to control data and program

diskettes, labeling the diskettes, where to store them, backup procedures, use of the computer, training, and recovery of costs are common to all businesses. But to the accounting firm the first six issues are magnified by the number of people who have access to the diskettes and the computers.

As far as we can tell, no one has come up with the perfect method for dealing with these problems. But don't give up yet. In the next section we will discuss how some accountants (including ourselves) are dealing with these inconveniences. The categories are broken down into four major areas: control of the diskettes, control of the computer, training, and recovery of costs.

Control of the Diskettes

I. Establish a library system with a permanent librarian in charge.
(The functions of the librarian are proposed as follows:)
   A. Tracking program diskettes
      1. Make a copy of the original program diskettes for everyday use.
      2. Keep a record of the original program diskettes and where they are stored.
      3. Keep a record of the copies of the program diskettes and where they are stored when not in use.
      4. Maintain an in and out log to track the location of the working copies of the program diskettes while they are in use.
   B. Inventory of diskettes
      1. Assign an inventory to new diskettes as received. Log them in.
      2. Format the diskettes so they will be ready for immediate use.
      3. Place a blank label on each diskette after formatting. This, at the very least, encourages proper labeling of diskettes by your staff—no more excuses about not being able to find a label. Be sure your staff knows to use only a felt-tip marker when labeling diskettes (to keep from damaging the surface of the magnetic media).
      4. Keep a log of the diskettes by inventory number. Note the date signed out, to whom, purpose, date of

return or disposal, and where the diskette will be stored.

C. Storage of diskettes
   1. Some accountants keep a copy of the client's workpaper diskette in with the client's workpaper file. A record of the inventory number of diskettes used on the job and where they are stored is also kept so that the diskettes can be updated and kept current. The record is also kept in the workpaper file with the diskette.
   2. A copy of the current workpaper diskette is kept in a central storage area as backup.

Control of Computer

Given that a firm has a limited number of computers available and what seems like an unlimited number of people who want to use them (or conversely, the same people want to use them all of the time), how do you control who uses them? Listed below are several ideas we have heard voiced at one time or another.

1. Lock the computer up. This is not very effective for productivity.
2. Buy a computer for each person. Very expensive.
3. Place the computer(s) and printer(s) in a specially designated area (the "computer room") permanently. This makes sense. Computers, like other office equipment, become proprietary when placed in someone's office or work area.
4. Place the computers in specially designated areas throughout the office. For example, the tax department would have two computers for its staff's exclusive use. Not a bad idea, but again, the computer(s) needs to be on neutral ground.
5. For portable computers, maintain a log and require your staff to sign in and out when using the portables outside of the office.

Training

We have already covered the subject of training as it relates to the actual machine and software (see Chapter 4). The area covered here is administrative procedures. Your staff has to be instructed in the proper procedures for handling diskettes (i.e., labeling, avoiding writing on the diskettes with sharp-tipped pencils and pens, backup, and storage) that your firm has set up.

Your word processing department will have different requirements than the professional staff. Here you must make a decision about how you will keep track of the diskettes with correspondence and reports on them, and what the backup procedures will be. The storage system can be broken down into categories. You may want to assign a diskette to each client, and only save that client's correspondence and reports to that diskette. You may also require diskettes for the firm's correspondence or a diskette with nothing on it but form letters. In any event, it is an organizational task, one that has to be figured out before you find yourself with two hundred diskettes with varying degrees of information on them.

Recovery of Costs

This topic covers the ongoing (as opposed to the training and startup costs covered earlier) costs of operating the computer. Such questions arise as, Should the client be charged for the cost of the diskettes and other expenses peculiar to computers? and Should a charge be attached to the use of the computer for client work? There is no one answer to these questions. Some accountants charge a flat fee for setup on the computer, some charge for computer supplies, and some charge for the use of the computer.

A.4 AFTER YOU ARE UP TO SPEED

Once you get to know a good accounting program, you will find it easier to set up. Each time you use it, there will be less trial-and-error learning. Even if a business has a good accounting staff, they will have a hard time learning the package before using it. And if they don't have anyone strong in accounting, then they will need some training in bookkeeping skills in order to run their new micro-accounting system.

It's a good idea to build a working relationship with one or more local computer stores. They are beginning to appreciate that the availability of some local micro-accounting expertise can help their sales. Potential customers are more easily assured that they are getting the right system for their needs and that they will be able to get as much support as they may need.

Billing for the Support

Businesses are willing to pay for such support separately from the system purchase price; in fact, they expect that approach everywhere except with microcomputer software. Those who want to "do-it-yourself" should just pay the price of the software; those who want to avoid that struggle should have that option available. The microcomputer industry is still recovering from the days when every user was a do-it-yourselfer.

Work with some local computer dealers to select one or two brands of accounting software that are acceptable to both you and them. You will have to learn that software in depth if you are to help new users convert their systems. The dealer will have to learn how to qualify customers. This means not selling the accounting system to customers unless it is the right answer to their needs. For some brands of software, only the dealers are allowed to call in and ask questions for end-users. Since your clients will always call you with their questions, it is best to find a software company that will respond to your calls.

Don't expect your clients to pay for your system and your learning. Most of them can't afford to pay one and a half times the purchase price of the computer just to get their accounting onto the computer. Your system should pay for itself from your internal uses of it (increased productivity, increased billable services, and so on), just like your typewriters and copiers. Also try to minimize the amount of learning at clients' offices. Clients with new computers are easily demoralized if they see their outside experts struggling to make the new system go. Your first few conversions will involve struggles, but do it back at your office, and exercise good judgment on what is billable and what is not.

Accounting Firms as Dealers

Here we question the idea of accounting firms becoming software dealers. There is definitely some money that can be made here, almost 50 percent of the list price of each software package. But it is not as easy as it sounds.

You have to pay a significant amount to each software house to become one of their authorized dealers. You will be expected to commit to buying a certain number of each module over the next 12 months and to provide a certain amount of free support for each system sold. You would then have trouble drawing the line between support that comes with the package and support that should be paid for. Some dealership arrangements require storefront displays and/or cooperative advertising campaigns.

You would face some very heavy competition. The same store that sells your clients their hardware and non-accounting software will be competing. There are many mail-order and discount software houses out there, and their prices are very close to what you as a dealer pay for the software. What do you say when clients ask why they should buy the software from you when they can get it for 50 percent less just down the way?

And then there is the conflict of interest argument. How can your clients be sure you are offering advice in their best interests if certain recommendations will make you some extra money? Being a dealer ties you to that brand. What will you do when some better software appears on the market?

APPENDIX B
TEXT BIBLIOGRAPHY

1. *Accountants' Guide to Computer Systems,* William E. Perry. New York: John Wiley & Sons, Inc., 1982.
2. *Computers for Small Business,* Gary Bencar. Santa Barbara, California: La Cumbre Publishing Company, 1983.
3. *Developing Computer Solutions for Your Business Problems,* Henry H. Petersohn. New Jersey: Prentice-Hall, Inc., 1982.
4. *A Guide for Selecting Computers and Software for Small Businesses,* Paul G. Enockson. Reston, Virginia: Reston Publishing Company, 1983.
5. *How to Buy a Business Computer and Get It Right the First Time,* Edward M. Cross. Reston, Virginia: Reston Publishing Company, 1983.
6. *How to Buy Software,* by Alfred Glossbrenner. New York: St. Martin's Press. An excellent guide.
7. *How to Find and buy Good Software,* Jess W. Curry and David M. Bonner. New Jersey: Prentice-Hall, Inc., 1983. A good 8-step strategy for selection and purchase.
8. *How to Microcomputerize Your Business,* Jules A. Cohen, Catherine S. Mckinney and the Staff of Orbis. New Jersey: Prentice-Hall, Inc., 1983.
9. *The IBM PC & Business Software,* James E. Kelly, Jr. Wayne, Pennsylvania: Banbury Books, 1983. Includes 2 floppy diskettes.
10. *Microcomputers for Accountants,* Theodore Needleman. New Jersey: Prentice-Hall, Inc., 1983. An excellent book for accountants.
11. *Microcomputers in Large Organizations,* Thomas William Madron. New Jersey: Prentice-Hall, Inc., 1983.
12. *Microcomputers in Small Businesses,* Robert D. Randall. New Jersey: Prentice-Hall, Inc., 1982.
13. *The Personal Computer in Business Book,* Peter A. McWilliams. Los Angeles, California: Prelude Press, 1983. A good introduction to PCs.
14. *A Practical Guide to Small Computers for Business and Professional Use,* Robert M. Rinder. New York: Monarch Press, 1981.
15. *Profitable Small Business Computing,* Frank Greenwood, edited by Gerald M. Weinberg. Boston: Little, Brown and Company, 1982.
16. *Simplified Guide to Small Computers for Business,* Daniel R. McGlynn. New York: John Wiley & Sons, Inc., 1983.

17. *So You Think You Need Your Own Business Computer*, William E. Perry. New York: John Wiley & Sons, Inc., 1982.

18. *The Software Sifter; an Intelligent Shopper's Guide to Buying Computer Software*, Philip Frankel and Ann Gras. New York: Macmillan Publishing Company, 1983. An excellent set of criteria lists for most types of software; little text.

19. *Using Micro-Computers in Business*, 2nd edition, Stanley S. Veit. Rochelle Park, New Jersey: Hayden Book Company, 1983.

20. *Your First Business Computer*, Peter and Rainer Luedtke. Bedford, Massachusetts: Digital Press, 1983.

APPENDIX C
MAGAZINE BIBLIOGRAPHY

1. *Business Computing Magazine*
   119 Russell Street
   Littleton, MA 01460
   (617) 486-9501

2. *BYTE Magazine*
   McGraw-Hill Inc.
   70 Main Street
   Peterborough, NH 03458
   (603) 924-9281

3. *Computer Currents*
   2550 Ninth Street
   Berkeley, CA 94710
   (415) 848-6860

4. *Computers In Accounting*
   964 Third Avenue
   New York, NY 10155
   (212) 935-9210

5. *Computer+Software News*
   Lebhar-Friedman Inc.
   425 Park Avenue
   New York, NY 10022
   (212) 371-9400

6. *InfoWorld Magazine*
   1060 Marsh Road, Suite C-200
   Menlo Park, CA 94025
   (415) 328-4602

7. *Interface Age Magazine*
   16704 Marquardt Avenue
   Cerritos, CA 90701
   (213) 926-9544

8. *Journal of Financial Software*
   Microthought Publications
   2811 Wilshire Boulevard
   Santa Monica, CA 90403
   (213) 829-7385

9. *Micro MarketWorld*
   1060 Marsh Road
   Menlo Park, CA 94025
   (415) 329-8220

10. *PC Magazine*
    One Park Avenue
    New York, NY 10016
    (212) 725-4694
11. *PC Week*
    15 Crawford Street
    Needham, MA 02194
    (617) 449-6520
12. *PC World*
    555 De Haro Street
    San Francisco, CA 94107
    (415) 861-3861
13. *Softalk-PC*
    7250 Laurel Canyon Boulevard
    North Hollywood, CA 91605
    (818) 980-5074
14. *UNIX/World*
    289 South San Antonio Road
    Los Altos, CA 94022
    (415) 949-3737

APPENDIX D
SOFTWARE BIBLIOGRAPHY

Company Names	Software Products
Accountants Microsystems, Inc. 3633 136th Place SE Bellevue, WA 98006 (206) 643-2050	AMI DATAWRITE (for accounting firms)
Amcom, Data Processing Services 464 McCormick Street San Leandro, CA 94577 (415) 638-1212	Amcom Accounting
American Business Systems, Inc. 3 Littleton Road Westford, MA 01886 (617) 692-2600	ABS Accounting
Apple Computer 20525 Mariani Avenue Cupertino, CA 95014 (408) 996-1010	
Armor Systems, Inc. 324 N. Orlando Avenue Maitland, FL 32751 (305) 629-0753	Excalibur Accounting
Automation Management, Inc. 5718 Westheimer, Suite 410 Houston, TX 77057 (713) 781-5941	SoftTouch Accounting
BPI Systems, Inc. 3423 Guadalupe Austin, TX 78705 (512) 454-2801	BPI Accounting
Bristol Information Systems, Inc. 84 North Main Street Fall River, MA 02720 (617) 679-1051	BIS Accounting

Company Names	Software Products
California Software Products, Inc. 525 North Cabrillo Park Drive Suite 300 Santa Ana, CA 92701 (714) 973-0440	BABY/34—runs IBM S/34 programs on a PC. (for accounting firms)
Cdex 5050 El Camino Real Los Altos, CA 94022 (415) 964-7600	Training programs
PLB, Incorporated Main Line Industrial Park Lee Boulevard Frazer, PA 19355 (215) 644-3344	Solomon III Accounting
Coopers & Lybrand 1251 Avenue of the Americas New York, NY 10020 (212) 536-2000	Tax and Audit programs
CYMA/McGraw-Hill 2160 East Brown Road Mesa, AZ 85203 (602) 835-8880	CYMA General Business Series
DSS Development Corporate Place 4 Barnard Lane Bloomfield, CT 06002 (203) 243-5554	Optionaware (for Lotus 1-2-3)
Financier, Inc. 2000 West Park Drive P.O. Box 670 Westboro, MA 01581 (617) 366-0950	Tax planning
Great Plains Software P.O. Box 9739 Fargo, ND 58102 (701) 281-0550	Hard disk Accounting

Company Names	Software Products
Hayden Software P.O. Box 8428 600 Suffolk Street Lowell, MA 01853 (617) 937-0200	Simplicity Accounting
Heritage Computing, Inc. 611 Anton Boulevard Suite 720 Costa Mesa, CA 92626 CA (714) 662-6999 (800) 227-3283	Jewel Accounting
Hewlett-Packard Personal Office Computer Division P.O. Box 486 974 E. Arques Avenue Sunnyvale, CA 94086 (408) 257-7000	
Information Unlimited Software, Inc. 2401 Marinship Way Sausalito, CA 94965 (415) 331-6700	IUS EasyBusiness Series
Insoft, Inc. P.O. Box 19208 Portland, OR 97219 (503) 244-4181	Insoft Accounting
Intellectual Software 798 North Avenue Bridgeport, CT 06606 1-800-232-2224 (203) 335-0906	Accounting training
International Micro Systems 6445 Metcalf Shawnee Mission, KS 66202 (913) 677-1137	IMS Accounting
ITM 2835 Mitchell Drive Walnut Creek, CA 94598 (800) 334-3404 (415) 947-0850	On-line software catalog Discount sales

Company Names	**Software Products**
Lotus Development Corporation 161 First Street Cambridge, MA 02142 (617) 492-7171	Lotus 1-2-3 [spreadsheet] Symphony
MAI/Basic Four Business Products Corp. 601 San Pedro N.E. Albuqerque, NM 87108 (505) 266-5811	MAI Accounting
Management Control Systems, Inc. 2400 Lake Park Drive Atlanta, GA 30339 (800) 241-3306	MCS Practice Mgmt. (for accounting firms) MCS General Accounting
MCBA 2441 Honolulu Avenue Montrose, CA 91020 (818) 957-2900	MCBA Accounting
McGraw-Hill 1020 North Broadway Milwaukee, WI 53202 (414) 289-9988	Aardvark tax planning
Micro Associates, Inc. 2300 Hwy 365 Nederland, TX 77627 (409) 724-6583	MICA Accounting
Micro Business Applications, Inc. 12281 Nicollet Avenue South Burnsville, MN 55337 (612) 894-3470	MBA Accounting
Microfinancial Corporation 15404 E. Valley Boulevard Industry, CA 91746 (213) 961-0237	Flexware Accounting
Microsoft Corporation 10700 Northup Way Bellevue, WA 98004 (206) 828-8080	MS/DOS operating system

Company Names	Software Products
Champion Software Corporation 66 South Van Gordon, Suite 155 Lakewood, CO 80228 (303) 987-2588	Champion Accounting
Open Systems 430 Oak Grove Minneapolis, MN 55403 (612) 870-3515	Software Fitness Accounting
Peachtree Software Incorporated 3445 Peachtree Road, N.E. Atlanta, GA 30326 (404) 239-3000	Peachtree General Accounting PeachPak-4
Pearlsoft P.O. Box 638 Wilsonville, OR 97070 (503) 682-3636	Accounting Pearl
Prentice-Hall, Inc. General Publishing Division Englewood Cliffs, NJ 07632 (201) 592-3314	Profit Center Accounting
Production Data Systems 2386 Fair Oaks Boulevard Sacramento, CA 95825 (916) 484-0155	TAJ Accounting
RealWorld Micro Business Software, Inc. Dover Road Chichester, NH 03263 (603) 798-5700	RealWorld Accounting RealWorld Bookkeeping
SMC Software Systems 1011 Route 22 Bridgewater, NJ 08807 (201) 685-9000 (800) 526-3968	
Software Dimensions, Inc. 100 Blue Ravine Road P.O. Box 1100 Folsom, CA 95630 (916) 985-6555	Accounting Plus

Company Names	Software Products
Software International One Tech Drive Andover, MA 01810 1-800-343-4133	
Business Library Corporation 2990 Bay Vista Court Benicia, CA 94510 CA (800) 451-1783 (800) 221-1985	The Business Library
Solid Software, Inc. 5500 Interstate North Parkway Suite 501 Atlanta, GA 30328 (404) 952-7709	Solid Accounting
SOLVation, Inc. 150 Flanders Road Westboro, MA 01581 (617) 366-6621	Small Business Accounting
Star Software Systems 20600 Gramercy Place Torrance, CA 90501 (213) 538-2511	Star General Accounting The Accounting Partner
State of the Art, Inc. 3183-A Airway Avenue Costa Mesa, CA 92626 (714) 850-0111	General Accounting The Bookkeeping System
Systems Plus, Inc. 1120 San Antonio Road Palo Alto, CA 94303 (415) 969-7047	BOOKS!
TCS Software, Inc. 3209 Fondren Houston, TX 77063 (713) 977-7505	TCS Total Accounting
Timberline P.O. Box 230120 Portland, OR 97223 (503) 644-8155	Medallion Accounting

APPENDIX E
WORKSHEETS AND CHECKLISTS

FIGURE 2.2

COST/BENEFIT ANALYSIS (ACCOUNTING ONLY)

Costs

Item	*Estimated Cost*
1. One-time costs:	
a. Computer(s)	$______
b. Printer(s)	______
c. Software	______
d. Furniture	______
e. Computer system training	______
f. Consulting—selection	______
—accounting installation	______
Subtotal	______
2. Divide by three to get annualized cost. assuming a three-year life for the system	______
3. Annual costs	
a. Supplies	______
b. Maintenance	______
c. Insurance	______
4. Subtotal (2+3)	______

5. If bringing accounting in-house from an outside accounting service, add these additional costs (only for the relevant accounting functions). First there are the additional labor requirements. Enter an estimate of the number of labor-hours it would take per month to manually do that part of your books. Then enter the average cost per hour of your bookkeeping staff.

General ledger:	____ hrs/mo × ____ $/hr × 12mo × 50% =	______
Accts rec:	____ hrs/mo × ____ $/hr × 12mo × 25% =	______
Accts payable:	____ hrs/mo × ____ $/hr × 12mo × 50% =	______
Payroll:	____ hrs/mo × ____ $/hr × 12mo × 25% =	______

FIGURE 2.2 (con.)

COST/BENEFIT ANALYSIS (ACCOUNTING ONLY)
Costs

Item | *Estimated Cost*

There will also be some additional training required. Figure on about one month's staff cost per module (just use the hrs/mo and $/hr figures from above).

General ledger:	___ hrs/mo × ___ $/hr =	________
Accts rec:	___ hrs/mo × ___ $/hr =	________
Accts payable:	___ hrs/mo × ___ $/hr =	________
Payroll:	___ hrs/mo × ___ $/hr =	________
Subtotal		________

6. Divide by three to get annualized cost, assuming a three-year life for the system. ________

7. Total annual cost (lines 2, 4, and 6 if appropriate) ________

FIGURE 2.3

COST/BENEFIT ANALYSIS (ACCOUNTING ONLY)
BENEFITS—IF CONVERTING FROM MANUAL TO MICRO

Estimated $ Benefit

1. Overall:
   a. Growth handled smoothly $________
   b. Reports available on a more timely basis ________
   c. No more arithmetic mistakes ________

2. General Ledger:
   a. Reduce the general ledger labor requirement:
      ___hrs/mo × ___ $/hr × 12mo × 50% = ________
   b. Better control of your business:
      - tailored reports—you can target data ________
      - summary status of business always available ________
      - details of accounts always available ________
      - period closings and financial statements available within a week or two ________
      - aids in keeping books in balance ________

FIGURE 2.3 (con.)

COST/BENEFIT ANALYSIS (ACCOUNTING ONLY) BENEFITS—IF CONVERTING FROM MANUAL TO MICRO

Estimated $ Benefit

3. Accounts Receivable:
   a. Improve bad debt ratio by 0.5%
      ______________ × 0.05 = ______________
      Total annual accounts receivable
   b. Reduce average A/R by 10% (and reinvest)
      ______________ × 0.1 × 0.08 = ______________
      Average accounts receivable interest rate
   c. Reduce accounts receivable labor requirements
      ______ hrs/mo × ______ $/hr × 12mo × 75% = ______________
   d. You can see detail/history on any customer at any time ______________
   e. Analysis of who buys what, when, and how they pay ______________

4. Accounts Payable:
   a. Reduce accounts payable labor requirements
      ______ hrs/mo × ______ $/hr × 12mo × 50% = ______________
   b. Better cash flow management:
      - see what you owe and when it is due ______________
      - track the value of discounts lost ______________
      - see where you stand with each vendor ______________
      - be able to monitor each bill separately ______________

5. Payroll:
   a. Reduce payroll labor requirements
      ______ hrs/mo × ______ $/hr × 12mo × 75% = ______________

6. Total Annual Benefit $______________

FIGURE 2.4

COST/BENEFIT ANALYSIS (ACCOUNTING ONLY)
BENEFITS—IF CONVERTING FROM OUTSIDE SERVICE TO MICRO

	Estimated $ Benefit
1. Overall:	
a. Your business records not sent off premises	
– they remain available	$ ________
– confidentiality remains under your control	________
b. Reports available on a more timely basis	________
c. Downtime and data losses under your control	________
d. No more telephone/mail/messenger fees	________
2. General Ledger:	
a. Reduction of outside service fees:	
______ $/mo × 12mo	________
3. Accounts receivable:	
a. Reduction of outside service fees:	
______ $/mo × 12mo	________
4. Accounts payable:	
a. Reduction of outside service fees:	
______ $/mo × 12mo	________
5. Payroll:	
a. Reduction of outside service fees:	
______ $/mo × 12mo	________
6. Total Annual Benefits	$ ________

FIGURE 3.6

REQUIREMENTS/EVALUATION LIST—OVERALL SYSTEM

Support	**R***	**D***	**DC***
1. Evaluation	[ ]	[ ]	[ ]
a. can find the information needed	[ ]	[ ]	[ ]
b. sample reports provided	[ ]	[ ]	[ ]
c. current users to talk to	[ ]	[ ]	[ ]
2. Demonstrations satisfactory	[ ]	[ ]	[ ]
3. Tutorials and sample data adequate	[ ]	[ ]	[ ]
4. Manuals clear, complete, easy to use	[ ]	[ ]	[ ]
5. Training provided			
a. on computer use	[ ]	[ ]	[ ]
b. on accounting software	[ ]	[ ]	[ ]
6. After-sales support: Who provides it? At what costs?	[ ]	[ ]	[ ]
a. local dealer	[ ]	[ ]	[ ]
b. regional distributor	[ ]	[ ]	[ ]
c. software publisher	[ ]	[ ]	[ ]
7. Returns policy	[ ]	[ ]	[ ]
Ease of Use			
8. Are the setup instructions clear?	[ ]	[ ]	[ ]
9. Rate the data entry/posting operations (try it!)	[ ]	[ ]	[ ]
10. Rate the backing up operations	[ ]	[ ]	[ ]
11. Are the end-of-period closing instructions/demo. clear?	[ ]	[ ]	[ ]
Features			
12. Number of accounting periods (per year):______	[ ]	[ ]	[ ]

(con.)

FIGURE 3.6 (con.)

REQUIREMENTS/EVALUATION LIST—OVERALL SYSTEM

Features	R*	D*	DC*
13. Can start new period before closing the old period	[ ]	[ ]	[ ]
14. Printer size:			
a. number of columns required:______	[ ]	[ ]	[ ]
b. supports compressed characters mode	[ ]	[ ]	[ ]
15. Can transfer accounting data to spreadsheet or database program?			
16. List any exceptional features desired.			
Security			
17. Describe the access controls for the PC system. (in detail or satisfactory/unsatisfactory, as desired)			
18. Describe the access controls for the accounting operations.			
19. Batch system?	[ ]	[ ]	[ ]
20. Allows editing/deletions			
a. of active account numbers	[ ]	[ ]	[ ]
b. of active account balances	[ ]	[ ]	[ ]
c. of posted transactions	[ ]	[ ]	[ ]
21. Allows out-of-balance condition	[ ]	[ ]	[ ]
Long-Term Considerations			
22. List the computers and operating systems it will run on. (Will this limit your expansion options later?)			
23. Third-party support, both programmers and developers of hardware accessories—this is an indication of acceptance and thus compatibility with future developments.			

* R = Required
* D = Desired
* DC = Don't Care

FIGURE 3.7

REQUIREMENTS/EVALUATION LIST—GENERAL LEDGER

Capacities	R*	D*	DC*
1. Account number structure:			
a. alphanumeric	[ ]	[ ]	[ ]
b. number of digits in main account number:______	[ ]	[ ]	[ ]
c. number of subaccount (department) digits:______	[ ]	[ ]	[ ]
d. number of characters in description:______	[ ]	[ ]	[ ]
2. Number of accounts in your chart of accounts:______	[ ]	[ ]	[ ]
a. number range of assets		______ to ______	
b. number range of liabilities		______ to ______	
c. number range of equity accounts		______ to ______	
d. number range of income accounts		______ to ______	
e. number range of cost of goods sold		______ to ______	
f. number range of expenses		______ to ______	
3. Number of journal entries:			
a. per batch:______	[ ]	[ ]	[ ]
b. per period:______	[ ]	[ ]	[ ]
4. Number of companies to be handled:______	[ ]	[ ]	[ ]
5. Number of departments to be handled:______	[ ]	[ ]	[ ]
6. Number of journals to be handled:______	[ ]	[ ]	[ ]
7. Maximum transaction amount			$______
8. Maximum total amount to be handled			$______
Reports			
9. Types of statements desired:			
a. balance sheet	[ ]	[ ]	[ ]
b. balance sheet with prior year comparisons	[ ]	[ ]	[ ]
c. income statement	[ ]	[ ]	[ ]
d. income statement with departmental income statement	[ ]	[ ]	[ ]
e. income statement with monthly budget comparisons	[ ]	[ ]	[ ]

FIGURE 3.7 (con.)

REQUIREMENTS/EVALUATION LIST—GENERAL LEDGER

Reports	R*	D*	DC*
f. income statement with prior year comparisons	[ ]	[ ]	[ ]
g. statement of changes in financial position	[ ]	[ ]	[ ]
h. subsidiary schedules to financial statements (for additional details)	[ ]	[ ]	[ ]
i. other custom reports	[ ]	[ ]	[ ]
10. Number of different formats desired for each financial statement: ______	[ ]	[ ]	[ ]
11. Additional special reports or schedules desired	[ ]	[ ]	[ ]
12. Flexibility:			
a. formats fixed	[ ]	[ ]	[ ]
b. formats by assigning each account a type	[ ]	[ ]	[ ]
c. allows multiple formats	[ ]	[ ]	[ ]
13. Chart of accounts printout fits your needs	[ ]	[ ]	[ ]
14. Trial balance worksheet format meets your needs	[ ]	[ ]	[ ]
15. General ledger:			
a. format meets your needs	[ ]	[ ]	[ ]
b. separate report for each period	[ ]	[ ]	[ ]
c. multi-period detail in one report	[ ]	[ ]	[ ]
16. Reports displayed or printed:			
a. all go only to printer	[ ]	[ ]	[ ]
b. individual account inquiries to screen	[ ]	[ ]	[ ]
c. some reports to screen	[ ]	[ ]	[ ]
d. any report can be displayed to screen	[ ]	[ ]	[ ]
Features			
17. Accounting basis:			
a. cash	[ ]	[ ]	[ ]
b. accrual	[ ]	[ ]	[ ]
18. Number of capital accounts possible	[ ]	[ ]	[ ]

FIGURE 3.7 (con.)

REQUIREMENTS/EVALUATION LIST—GENERAL LEDGER

Features	R*	D*	DC*
19. Automatic posting of recurring entries (e.g., depreciation)	[ ]	[ ]	[ ]
20. Automatic allocation of expenses	[ ]	[ ]	[ ]
21. Automatic reversing of journal entries	[ ]	[ ]	[ ]
22. Correcting entries postable			
a. to prior period	[ ]	[ ]	[ ]
b. to prior year	[ ]	[ ]	[ ]
23. List any exceptional features.			

* R = Required
* D = Desired
* DC = Don't Care

FIGURE 3.8

REQUIREMENTS/EVALUATION LIST—ACCOUNTS RECEIVABLE

Capacities	*R	*D	*DC
1. Customer number structure:			
a. alphanumeric	[ ]	[ ]	[ ]
b. number of digits in customer body:______	[ ]	[ ]	[ ]
c. number of characters in description:______	[ ]	[ ]	[ ]
2. Other customer information to be accumulated	[ ]	[ ]	[ ]
3. Number of accounts receivable control accounts in your general ledger:______	[ ]	[ ]	[ ]
4. Number of general ledger accounts referenced by the accounts receivable module:______	[ ]	[ ]	[ ]
5. Number of recurring entries:______	[ ]	[ ]	[ ]

FIGURE 3.8 (con.)

REQUIREMENTS/EVALUATION LIST—ACCOUNTS RECEIVABLE

Capacities	**R***	**D***	**DC***
6. Number of one-time customers per period:______ (cash sales and miscellaneous receipts)	[ ]	[ ]	[ ]
7. Number of customers to whom you extend credit:______	[ ]	[ ]	[ ]
8. Number of invoices			
a. per batch:______	[ ]	[ ]	[ ]
b. per period:______	[ ]	[ ]	[ ]
9. Number of invoice payments			
a. per batch:______	[ ]	[ ]	[ ]
b. per period:______	[ ]	[ ]	[ ]
10. Maximum transaction amount			$______
11. Maximum total amount to be handled			$______
12. Number of lines per invoice:______	[ ]	[ ]	[ ]
13. Number of lines per statement:______	[ ]	[ ]	[ ]
Reports			
14. Aging report:			
a. summary	[ ]	[ ]	[ ]
b. detail	[ ]	[ ]	[ ]
c. all customers	[ ]	[ ]	[ ]
d. past-due customers	[ ]	[ ]	[ ]
e. sorted/selected by other criteria (e.g., amount)	[ ]	[ ]	[ ]
f. on-screen inquiries	[ ]	[ ]	[ ]
15. Customer roster:			
a. alphabetical	[ ]	[ ]	[ ]
b. numerical	[ ]	[ ]	[ ]
c. other (by zip code, etc.)	[ ]	[ ]	[ ]
d. mailing labels	[ ]	[ ]	[ ]

FIGURE 3.8 (con.)

REQUIREMENTS/EVALUATION LIST—ACCOUNTS RECEIVABLE

Reports	R*	D*	DC*
16. Prints invoices	[ ]	[ ]	[ ]
a. extends amounts	[ ]	[ ]	[ ]
b. calculates sales tax	[ ]	[ ]	[ ]
c. ship-to address	[ ]	[ ]	[ ]
17. Statements	[ ]	[ ]	[ ]
a. suppresses those with zero balances	[ ]	[ ]	[ ]
b. messages possible	[ ]	[ ]	[ ]
18. Sales analysis:			
a. by sales representative	[ ]	[ ]	[ ]
b. by sales territory	[ ]	[ ]	[ ]
19. Summary journal entries	[ ]	[ ]	[ ]
20. Detail journal entries	[ ]	[ ]	[ ]
21. Customer ledger	[ ]	[ ]	[ ]
Features			
22. Receivable types:			
a. open item (payment against specific invoices)	[ ]	[ ]	[ ]
b. balance forward (payments against balance)	[ ]	[ ]	[ ]
c. can be changed easily at any time	[ ]	[ ]	[ ]
23. Aging periods:			
a. selectable	[ ]	[ ]	[ ]
b. including future amounts due	[ ]	[ ]	[ ]
24. Automatic posting of recurring charges	[ ]	[ ]	[ ]
25. Credit memos	[ ]	[ ]	[ ]
26. Debit memos	[ ]	[ ]	[ ]
27. Finance charges	[ ]	[ ]	[ ]
a. with compounding	[ ]	[ ]	[ ]

FIGURE 3.8 (con.)

REQUIREMENTS/EVALUATION LIST—ACCOUNTS RECEIVABLE

Features	R*	D*	DC*
28. Discounts	[ ]	[ ]	[ ]
29. Partial payments	[ ]	[ ]	[ ]
30. Credit limit checking	[ ]	[ ]	[ ]
31. Cash sales and miscellaneous receipts	[ ]	[ ]	[ ]
32. Sales commissions computed	[ ]	[ ]	[ ]
a. number of different rates	[ ]	[ ]	[ ]
33. Late charges	[ ]	[ ]	[ ]
34. List any exceptional features.			

* R = Required
* D = Desired
* DC = Don't Care

FIGURE 3.9

REQUIREMENTS/EVALUATION LIST—ACCOUNTS PAYABLE

Capacities	R*	D*	DC*
1. Vendor number structure:			
a. alphanumeric	[ ]	[ ]	[ ]
b. number of digits in vendor number:______	[ ]	[ ]	[ ]
c. number of characters in description:______	[ ]	[ ]	[ ]
2. Other vendor information to be accumulated	[ ]	[ ]	[ ]
3. Number of accounts payable control accounts in your general ledger:______	[ ]	[ ]	[ ]
4. Number of general ledger control accounts referenced by the accounts payable module:______	[ ]	[ ]	[ ]
5. Number of recurring entries:______	[ ]	[ ]	[ ]
6. Number of one-time vendors per period:______	[ ]	[ ]	[ ]

FIGURE 3.9 (con.)

REQUIREMENTS/EVALUATION LIST—ACCOUNTS PAYABLE

Capacities	R*	D*	DC*
7. Number of invoices			
a. per batch:______	[ ]	[ ]	[ ]
b. per period:______	[ ]	[ ]	[ ]
8. Number of checks			
a. per batch:______	[ ]	[ ]	[ ]
b. per period:______	[ ]	[ ]	[ ]
9. Number of checking accounts:______	[ ]	[ ]	[ ]
10. Maximum invoice amount			$______
11. Maximum total amount to be handled			$______
12. Number of lines per voucher description (The voucher is the portion on the check where the invoice number and description is written.):______	[ ]	[ ]	[ ]
Reports			
13. Aging reports:			
a. summary	[ ]	[ ]	[ ]
b. detail	[ ]	[ ]	[ ]
c. all vendors	[ ]	[ ]	[ ]
d. selected vendors	[ ]	[ ]	[ ]
e. by due date	[ ]	[ ]	[ ]
f. by amount owed	[ ]	[ ]	[ ]
g. by other	[ ]	[ ]	[ ]
h. future amounts due	[ ]	[ ]	[ ]
i. on-screen inquiries	[ ]	[ ]	[ ]
14. Vendor roster:			
a. alphabetical	[ ]	[ ]	[ ]
b. numerical	[ ]	[ ]	[ ]
c. mailing labels	[ ]	[ ]	[ ]
15. Payment selection listing	[ ]	[ ]	[ ]

FIGURE 3.9 (con.)

REQUIREMENTS/EVALUATION LIST—ACCOUNTS PAYABLE

Reports	**R***	**D***	**DC***
16. Checks	[ ]	[ ]	[ ]
a. inhibits zero and negative amounts	[ ]	[ ]	[ ]
b. check "protector" pattern	[ ]	[ ]	[ ]
17. Check register	[ ]	[ ]	[ ]
a. flags breaks in the number sequence	[ ]	[ ]	[ ]
b. lists manually prepared checks	[ ]	[ ]	[ ]
c. notes voided checks	[ ]	[ ]	[ ]
18. Outstanding checks listing	[ ]	[ ]	[ ]
19. Discounts lost	[ ]	[ ]	[ ]
20. Vendor analysis	[ ]	[ ]	[ ]
21. Summary journal entries	[ ]	[ ]	[ ]
22. Detail journal entries	[ ]	[ ]	[ ]
23. Vendor ledger	[ ]	[ ]	[ ]
Features			
24. Payment selection options (who to pay):			
a. by vendor name	[ ]	[ ]	[ ]
b. by vendor number	[ ]	[ ]	[ ]
c. by due date	[ ]	[ ]	[ ]
d. by aging	[ ]	[ ]	[ ]
e. by invoice number	[ ]	[ ]	[ ]
f. by exception (pay all except. . .)	[ ]	[ ]	[ ]
25. Hold payment(s) option	[ ]	[ ]	[ ]
26. Reverse an invoice previously selected for payment	[ ]	[ ]	[ ]
27. Voided checks			
a. computer prepared	[ ]	[ ]	[ ]
b. manually prepared	[ ]	[ ]	[ ]

FIGURE 3.9 (con.)

REQUIREMENTS/EVALUATION LIST—ACCOUNTS PAYABLE

Features	R*	D*	DC*
28. Recurring checks	[ ]	[ ]	[ ]
29. Credit memos	[ ]	[ ]	[ ]
30. Debit memos	[ ]	[ ]	[ ]
31. Finance charges	[ ]	[ ]	[ ]
32. Discounts	[ ]	[ ]	[ ]
33. Discounts forced (past discount date)	[ ]	[ ]	[ ]
34. Partial payments	[ ]	[ ]	[ ]
35. Manually prepared checks	[ ]	[ ]	[ ]
36. One-time-only checks	[ ]	[ ]	[ ]
37. List any exceptional features.			

* R = Required
* D = Desired
* DC = Don't Care

FIGURE 3.10

REQUIREMENTS/EVALUATION LIST—PAYROLL

Capacities	R*	D*	DC*
1. Employee account number structure:			
a. alphanumeric	[ ]	[ ]	[ ]
b. number of digits in employee account number:______	[ ]	[ ]	[ ]
2. Employee information to be accumulated			
3. Number of payroll accounts in your general ledger:______	[ ]	[ ]	[ ]
4. Number of general ledger accounts referenced by the payroll module:______	[ ]	[ ]	[ ]
5. Number of permanent employees:______	[ ]	[ ]	[ ]

FIGURE 3.10 (con.)

REQUIREMENTS/EVALUATION LIST—PAYROLL

Capacities	R*	D*	DC*
6. Types of pay period(s) (semimonthly, etc.)	[ ]	[ ]	[ ]
7. Maximum paycheck amount			$______
8. Maximum total amount to be handled			$______
9. Maximum number of employees:______	[ ]	[ ]	[ ]
10. Number of optional deductions:______	[ ]	[ ]	[ ]
Reports			
11. Checks:			
a. fixed format	[ ]	[ ]	[ ]
b. flexible format	[ ]	[ ]	[ ]
12. Check register	[ ]	[ ]	[ ]
13. Employee roster	[ ]	[ ]	[ ]
14. Employee inquiry (all details)	[ ]	[ ]	[ ]
15. Wage reports (individual employee compensation records)	[ ]	[ ]	[ ]
16. Payroll summary	[ ]	[ ]	[ ]
17. Pre-check-printing report	[ ]	[ ]	[ ]
18. 1099s	[ ]	[ ]	[ ]
19. 941s	[ ]	[ ]	[ ]
20. W2s	[ ]	[ ]	[ ]
21. Checks	[ ]	[ ]	[ ]
a. inhibits zero and negative amounts	[ ]	[ ]	[ ]
b. check "protector" pattern	[ ]	[ ]	[ ]
22. Check register	[ ]	[ ]	[ ]
a. flags breaks in the number sequence	[ ]	[ ]	[ ]
b. lists manually prepared checks	[ ]	[ ]	[ ]
c. notes voided checks	[ ]	[ ]	[ ]

FIGURE 3.10 (con.)

REQUIREMENTS/EVALUATION LIST—PAYROLL

Reports	R*	D*	DC*
23. Summary journal entries	[ ]	[ ]	[ ]
24. Detail journal entries	[ ]	[ ]	[ ]
25. Outstanding checks listing	[ ]	[ ]	[ ]
Features			
26. Payroll types:			
a. hourly	[ ]	[ ]	[ ]
b. salaried	[ ]	[ ]	[ ]
c. commission	[ ]	[ ]	[ ]
d. other	[ ]	[ ]	[ ]
27. Supplemental pay:			
a. holiday	[ ]	[ ]	[ ]
b. vacation	[ ]	[ ]	[ ]
c. sick time	[ ]	[ ]	[ ]
d. other	[ ]	[ ]	[ ]
28. Manually prepared checks	[ ]	[ ]	[ ]
29. Voided checks:			
a. computer prepared	[ ]	[ ]	[ ]
b. manually prepared	[ ]	[ ]	[ ]
30. Automatic deductions:			
a. union fees	[ ]	[ ]	[ ]
b. loans	[ ]	[ ]	[ ]
c. garnishments	[ ]	[ ]	[ ]
d. health insurance	[ ]	[ ]	[ ]
e. other	[ ]	[ ]	[ ]
31. Worker's compensation calculations	[ ]	[ ]	[ ]
32. Terminated employees	[ ]	[ ]	[ ]
33. Inactive employees	[ ]	[ ]	[ ]
34. Pay advances	[ ]	[ ]	[ ]

FIGURE 3.10 (con.)

REQUIREMENTS/EVALUATION LIST—PAYROLL

Features	R*	D*	DC*
35. Withholding tables:			
a. entered and maintained by user	[ ]	[ ]	[ ]
b. supplied and updated by software publisher	[ ]	[ ]	[ ]
36. List any exceptional features.			

* R = Required
* D = Desired
* DC = Don't Care

FIGURE 4.1 General Ledger Conversion Checklist

I. Study current system.
   A. See Section 2.3, "Accounting Needs."

II. Design new system.
   A. Design chart of accounts.
      1. What departments will be involved (e.g., locations, branches, cost centers, profit centers)?
      2. What level of detail is desired (e.g., multiple sales accounts to show categories of sales or just one overall sales account)?
      3. Rewrite chart of accounts to include any changes.
   B. Design journals.
      1. What journals will be needed (e.g., cash receipts, cash disbursements, general journal)?
   C. Design reports.
      1. What types of reports are desired/needed?
         a. chart of accounts
         b. balance sheet
            (1) balance sheet with prior-year comparisons
         c. income statement
            (1) income statement with departmental income statements
            (2) income statement with monthly budget comparisons
            (3) income statement with prior-year comparisons
         d. statement of changes in financial position
         e. subsidiary schedules to financial statements (for additional detail)
         f. other custom reports
   D. Design password system.

III. Set up software structure (differs significantly between brands of software).
   A. Enter the new user information, such as company name and address, passwords, and sometimes type of printer, balance forward date, and so on.
   B. Enter the chart of accounts and balance forward amounts. (You will need a trial balance as of the balance forward date for the general ledger).
   C. Enter the desired report formats (if your program allows this to be done separately from the data entry procedure).
   D. Verify all of the data entered by printing out and proofing the appropriate reports. For example, the

chart of accounts, the general ledger, and the financial statements.

E. Make corrections as necessary.

IV. Gather and organize data.

A. For comparative reports, you will need a trial balance for each month (or quarter) that you will want to compare.

B. For monthly budgets, you will need a worksheet showing the monthly budget amounts for each account involved.

V. Data entry and verification

A. Use the above worksheets to enter the amounts.

B. Print out the appropriate reports and verify the amounts against the original worksheets.

C. Make corrections as necessary.

VI. Operator training (for day-to-day operations)

A. Formal training

1. Send employees to classes.
2. Training sessions with specialist (who knows that accounting software and is familiar with your accounting system)

B. Informal training

1. Tutorials
2. On-the-job training (from someone in the company who has been trained)
3. Discussion groups (to answer questions, allay fears, describe benefits)

VII. System testing and startup

A. Start entering transactions to appropriate journals, in parallel to your current system.

1. At the completion of the first accounting period (usually a month), print the journal entry listings, the general ledger, and the financial statements, and compare them to the manual system.
2. Locate the source of any discrepancies, and make adjustments.

VIII. Integration of modules

A. Be sure that each additional module is running correctly in a stand-alone mode before integrating it into the rest of your system.

B. Use an extra (duplicate diskette) copy of your accounting data (for the modules involved) to do a trial integration (i.e., do a parallel run to your computer system).

FIGURE 4.1 General Ledger Conversion Checklist (con.)

   C. Print out the appropriate reports and check the integration results.
   D. Locate the source of any problems, make adjustments, and try it again.
   E. Only when it is working correctly should you integrate your live system.

IX. Final documentation of your micro-accounting procedures
   A. As you start up your daily entry on the computer system, make notes as to how that entry is being performed (step by step, in detail, plus notes on common or anticipated errors, and how to recover from them).
   B. Compile the notes on the various operations into an organized document.
   C. Test the document by carrying out (on the computer) every step listed.

FIGURE 4.2 Accounts Receivable Conversion Checklist

I. Study current system.
   A. See Section 2.3, "Accounting Needs."

II. Design new system.
   A. Decide which method of receivables accounting you will be using, balance forward or open item, or both.
   B. Determine what, if any, recurring entries will be needed.
   C. Design customer number.
   D. Determine what information is to be accumulated on each customer.
   E. Design format of invoices and statements, if applicable to your software.
   F. Order invoices and statements to fit the new system.
   G. Design password system.

III. Set up software structure (differs significantly between brands of software).
   A. Enter the new user information, such as company name and address, passwords, and sometimes type of printer, balance forward date, and so on.
   B. Enter the desired report formats (if applicable).
   C. Verify all of the data entered by printing out and proofing the appropriate reports.
   D. Make corrections as necessary.

FIGURE 4.2 Accounts Receivable Conversion Checklist (con.)

IV. Gather and organize data.
  A. Determine the input form for setting up the receivables (what specific information and the order in which it will be needed).
  B. Locate the data items and determine how much gathering and compiling will be needed. You want to end up with just one sheet of information for each customer. You may be able to just use a current form and add a few numbers to it.
  C. For setting up the recurring entries, you will need to compile a list of customer numbers, customer names, amounts, and perhaps frequency.
  D. For setting up the terms codes and the product codes (if applicable), you will need to compile appropriate lists of those codes.

V. Data entry and verification
  A. Use the above worksheets to enter the amounts.
  B. Print out the appropriate reports and verify the amounts against the original worksheets.
  C. Make corrections as necessary.

VI. Operator training (for day-to-day operations)
  A. Formal training
    1. Send employees to classes.
    2. Training sessions with specialist (who knows that accounting software and is familiar with your accounting system)
  B. Informal training
    1. Tutorials
    2. On-the-job training (from someone in the company who has been trained)
    3. Discussion groups (to answer questions, allay fears, describe benefits)

VII. System startup and testing
  A. Start entering transactions in parallel to your current system.
    1. Note that your live invoices and statements should be coming from your manual system and that you should be printing facsimiles on plain white paper (if applicable to your software).
  B. At the completion of the first accounting period (usually a month), print the invoice register, the journal entry listings, the customer ledger, and other reports, and compare them to the manual system.
  C. Locate the source of any discrepancies and make adjustments.

FIGURE 4.2 Accounts Receivable Conversion Checklist (con.)

VIII. Integration of modules
  A. Be sure that each additional module is running correctly in a stand-alone mode before integrating it into the rest of your system.
  B. Use an extra (duplicate diskette) copy of your accounting data (for the modules involved) to do a trial integration (i.e., do a parallel run to your computer system).
  C. Print out the appropriate reports and check the integration results.
  D. Locate the source of any problems, make adjustments, and try it again.
  E. Only when it is working correctly should you integrate your live system.

IX. Final documentation of your micro-accounting procedures
  A. As you start up your daily entry on the computer system, make notes as to how that entry is being performed. (step by step, in detail, plus notes on common or anticipated errors and how to recover from them).
  B. Compile the notes on the various operations into an organized document.
  C. Test the document by carrying out every step listed.

FIGURE 4.3 Accounts Payable Conversion Checklist

I. Study current system.
  A. See Section 2.3, "Accounting Needs."

II. Design new system.
  A. Determine what, if any, recurring entries will be needed.
  B. Design vendor number.
  C. Determine what information is to be accumulated on each vendor.
  D. Design format of checks, if applicable to your software.
  E. Order checks to fit the new system.
  F. Determine password system.

III. Set up software structure (differs significantly between brands of software).
  A. Enter the new user information, such as company name and address, passwords, and, sometimes, type of printer, balance forward date, and so on.
  B. Enter the desired report formats (if applicable).

FIGURE 4.3 Accounts Payable Conversion Checklist (con.)

- C. Verify all of the data that has been entered, by printing out and proofing the appropriate reports.
- D. Make corrections as necessary.

IV. Gather and organize data.
- A. Determine the input form for setting up the payables (what specific information, and the order in which it will be needed).
- B. Locate the data items and determine how much gathering and compiling will be needed. You want to end up with just one sheet of information for each vendor. You may be able to just use a current form and add a few numbers to it.
- C. For setting up the recurring entries, you will need to compile a list of vendor numbers, names, amounts, and, perhaps, frequency.
- D. For setting up the terms codes, you will need to compile an appropriate list.

V. Data entry and verification
- A. Use the above worksheets to enter the amounts.
- B. Print out the appropriate reports and verify the amounts against the original worksheets.
- C. Make corrections as necessary.

VI. Operator training (for day-to-day operations)
- A. Formal training
  1. Send employees to classes.
  2. Training sessions with specialist (who knows that accounting software and is familiar with your accounting system)
- B. Informal training
  1. Tutorials
  2. On-the-job training (from someone in the company who has been trained)
  3. Discussion groups (to answer questions, allay fears, describe benefits)

VII. System testing and startup
- A. Start entering transactions, in parallel to your current system.
  1. Note that your live checks should be coming from your manual system and that you should be printing facsimiles on plain white paper.
- B. At the completion of the first accounting period (usually a month), print the check register, the journal entry listings, the vendor ledger, and other reports, and compare them to the manual system.
- C. Locate the source of any discrepancies and make adjustments.

FIGURE 4.3 Accounts Payable Conversion Checklist (con.)

VIII. Integration of modules
  A. Be sure that each additional module is running correctly in a stand-alone mode before integrating it into the rest of your system.
  B. Use an extra (duplicate diskette) copy of your accounting data (for the modules involved) to do a trial integration (i.e., do a parallel run to your computer system).
  C. Print out the appropriate reports and check the integration results.
  D. Locate the source of any problems, make adjustments, and try again.
  E. Only when it is working correctly should you integrate your live system.

IX. Final documentation of your micro-accounting procedures
  A. As you start up your daily entry on the computer system, make notes as to how that entry is being performed (step by step, in detail, plus notes on common or anticipated errors and how to recover from them).
  B. Compile the notes on the various operations into an organized document.
  C. Test the document by carrying out every step listed.

FIGURE 4.4 Payroll Conversion Checklist

I. Study current system.
  A. See Section 2.3, "Accounting Needs."

II. Design new system.
  A. Design employee numbers.
  B. Determine what information is to be accumulated on each employee.
  C. Determine the various non-tax deductions needed for the various employees and label them as required by the software.
  D. Determine which non-tax deductions are automatic.
  E. Design format of checks, if applicable to your software.
  F. Order checks to fit the new system.
  G. Determine password system.

III. Set up software structure (procedures differ significantly between brands of software).
  A. Enter the new user information, such as company name and address, passwords, and, sometimes, type of printer, balance forward date, and so on.

- B. Enter the desired report formats (if applicable).
- C. Verify all of the data that has been entered by printing out and proofing the appropriate reports.
- D. Make corrections as necessary.

IV. Gather and organize data.

- A. Determine the input form for setting up the employees (what specific information and the order in which it will be needed).
- B. Locate the data items and determine how much gathering and compiling will be needed. You want to end up with just one sheet of information for each employee. You may be able to just use a current form and add a few numbers to it.
- C. Compile the input forms.
- D. For setting up the tax tables (if not supplied within the software), you will need to compile a list of tables needed and gather together copies of those tables (as in the "Employer's Tax Guide," Circular E, from the Internal Revenue Service).

V. Data entry and verification

- A. Use the above worksheets and tax tables to enter the amounts.
- B. Print out the appropriate reports and verify the amounts against the original worksheets.
- C. Make corrections as necessary.

VI. Operator training (for day-to-day operations)

- A. Formal training
  1. Send employees to classes.
  2. Training sessions with specialist (who knows that accounting software and is familiar with your accounting system)
- B. Informal training
  1. Tutorials
  2. On-the-job training (from someone in the company who has been trained)
  3. Discussion groups (to answer questions, allay fears, describe benefits)

VII. System testing and startup

- A. Start entering transactions, in parallel to your current system.
  1. Note that your live payroll checks should be coming from your manual system and that you should be printing facsimiles on plain white paper.
- B. At the completion of the first payroll, print the payroll check register, the journal entry listings, the

FIGURE 4.4 Payroll Conversion Checklist (con.)

employee ledger, and other reports, and compare them to the manual system.

C. Locate the source of any discrepancies and make adjustments.

VIII. Integration of modules

A. Be sure that each additional module is running correctly in a stand-alone mode before integrating it into the rest of your system.

B. Use an extra (duplicate diskette) copy of your accounting data (for the modules involved) to do a trial integration (i.e., do a parallel run to your computer system).

C. Print out the appropriate reports and check the integration results.

D. Locate the source of any problems, make adjustments, and try again.

E. Only when it is working correctly should you integrate your live system.

IX. Final documentation of your micro-accounting procedures

A. As you start up your daily entry on the computer system, make notes as to how that entry is being performed (step by step, in detail, plus notes on common or anticipated errors and how to recover from them).

B. Compile the notes on the various operations into an organized document.

C. Test the document by carrying out every step listed.

APPENDIX F
SAMPLE FINAL DOCUMENTATION

ABC WATER COMPANY

ACCOUNTING PROCEDURES
FOR THE GENERAL LEDGER ACCOUNTING
SOFTWARE PROGRAM

KNIGHT & COMPANY
Certified Public Accountants

TABLE OF CONTENTS

GETTING STARTED

1. Take the *bring up* diskette and place it in diskette drive A. Close the door to the diskette drive.
2. Turn on the computer using the on/off switch located at the right rear side of the computer.
3. From the System Main Menu, select **F10**.
4. From the System Utilities Menu, select **F2**.
5. At the **C>** type in **GL** and press the return key.
6. Turn on the **Num Lock** key.
7. The accounting program will now ask for the current date. It is necessary to enter six digits for the date. For example, August 5, 1999, would be entered as 080599. You do not have to enter any slashes or dashes (i.e., 08/05/99). Press the return key.
8. When the **MASTER SELECTION GUIDE** appears, select item:

   `(A) General Ledger.`

9. Next you will be asked to enter your company code. Type in:

   `ABC`

10. You are now ready to select the operation you wish to perform from the **GENERAL LEDGER OPERATIONS GUIDE**.

ENTERING CASH RECEIPTS

1. From the GENERAL LEDGER OPERATIONS GUIDE, select item:

   `(C) Add, Delete or Change Journal Entries.`

   a. When the screen changes, select item:

      `(A) Add, Delete or Change Journal Entries.`

   b. Again the screen changes, asking you which journal to select:

      `Select Journal: [Enter] A.`

   c. You are now ready to enter the cash receipts data. The order of entry is as follows:

      (1) Enter the amount of the deposit first. This is the debit to cash. The screen looks like this:

Screen:	Comments:
Entry Number:	Assigned by the program
Entry Date:	Date of deposit to bank
Description:	Enter Deposit
Document:	Enter number from the deposit slip
Account:	Enter 120
Amount:	Enter total deposited

(See the sample deposit entry at page 213.)

(2) Next enter the amounts (checks) that make up the deposit. These are all credit amounts and must be preceded by a minus (−) sign. For the document description, use the number from the deposit slip. The account number to be credited will vary depending on the source of the cash receipt.

(See the sample cash receipt entry at page 214.)

2. Verifying cash receipts entries: When you have entered all cash receipts, the *Document Total* on the bottom of the screen should be the same as the total deposited to the bank. If it is not, then there is an inconsistency, and you will have to go back and view the entries made. To view the entries, select item **'V'—View Entries** (help messages are located at the bottom of the next screen), and press the return key. You will need to know the transaction number—just start with the number before your final entry for that day's deposit and work back. When you have located the mistake, note the transaction number on a piece of paper and go to the next screen. Select item **'C'—Change Entries** to correct the entry. When you have determined that the entries are correct, check the *Batch Total* amount and determine that it is zero. The Journal Total and Ledger Total should *always* be zero at the end of a data entry session. If they are not, perform the procedure described in the last paragraph before continuing.

You can change any entry up until the time you perform the posting function from the General Ledger Operations Guide. After you have posted, you may still make changes to any line *except* the account number line. (To change an account number after posting, you must delete the original entry and reenter it.)

3. Once you have verified that the entries balance, go back to the GENERAL LEDGER OPERATIONS GUIDE by entering an **'R'**—Return to General Ledger Operations and pressing the return key.

4. Now perform the posting function. From the GENERAL LEDGER OPERATIONS GUIDE, select item:

```
(D) Post Entries to Chart of Accounts.
```

(C) Add, Delete, or Change Journal Entries

ABC WATER COMPANY

CASH RECEIPTS (A)

Entry Number: 1

Entry Date: 080499
Description: DEPOSIT
Document: 2565
Account: 120
Amount: 3778.66

Document Total	Batch Total	Journal Total	Ledger Total
0.00	0.00	0.00	00.00

Enter Entry Number: <

This Option Will Allow You to View any Previous Entry

(C) Add, Delete, or Change Journal Entries

ABC WATER COMPANY

CASH RECEIPTS (A)

Entry Number: 231

Entry Date: 083199
Description: A/R COLLECTIONS
Document: CR
Account: 125
Amount: -36735.54

Document Total	Batch Total	Journal Total	Ledger Total
0.00	0.00	0.00	00.00

Enter Entry Number: <

This Option Will Allow You to View any Previous Entry

ENTERING CASH DISBURSEMENTS

1. Run an adding machine tape of the net check amounts for the checks you are entering. The total of this tape will be used later to verify against the total entered into the computer.

2. From the GENERAL LEDGER OPERATIONS GUIDE, select item:

    `(C) Add, Delete or Change Journal Entries.`

    a. When the screen changes, select item:

    `(A) Add, Delete or Change Journal Entries.`

    b. Again the screen changes, asking you which journal to select:

    `Select Journal: [Enter] B.`

    c. You are now ready to enter the cash disbursements data. The screen looks like this:

Screen:	Comments:
Entry Number:	Assigned by the program
Entry Date:	Date check was written
Description:	Payee
Document:	Check number
Account:	Varies with check
Amount:	May vary from net check

(1) Enter the debit side of all checks first. After you have finished entering all checks, compare the batch total to the adding machine tape total. If they do not agree, you must locate the difference before proceeding. It is easiest in this situation to run a listing of all of the check entries on the printer. Checks with multiple distribution can be verified using the *Document Total*, similar to that function's usage when entering cash receipts (see item 2, page 212).

(2) The credit side of the entry is made once for all checks using the minus (−) sign and is the same amount as was agreed between the Journal Total after the last debit entry was made and the adding machine tape. (See the sample entry at page 318.)

The Journal Total and Ledger Total should *always* be zero at the end of a data entry session. If they are not, perform the procedure described in the next-to-last paragraph before continuing.

You may change any entry up until the time you perform the posting function from the General Ledger Operations Guide. After you have posted, you may still make changes to any line *except* the account number line. (To change an account number after posting, you must delete the original entry and reenter it.)

To enter a *void check*, see page 317.

3. Once you have verified that the entries balance, go back to the GENERAL LEDGER OPERATIONS GUIDE by entering an **'R'—Return to General Ledger Operations** on the screen after your last entry and press the return key.

4. Now perform the posting function. From the GENERAL LEDGER OPERATIONS GUIDE, select item:

```
(D) Post Entries to Chart of Accounts.
```

```
(C) Add, Delete, or Change Journal Entries

              ABC WATER COMPANY

           CASH DISBURSEMENTS (A)

     Entry Number: 298

       Entry Date: 091599
      Description: VOID
         Document: 9999
          Account: 903.2 VOID CHECKS CLEARING
           Amount: 00          <

Document Total   Batch Total   Journal Total   Ledger Total
          0.00          0.00            0.00          00.00


        Enter 'F' to Fix Previous Question

    Press 'RETURN' to Copy Previous Information
```

```
                    (C) Add, Delete, or Change Journal Entries

                              ABC WATER COMPANY

                           CASH DISBURSEMENTS (B)

                 Entry Number: 190

                   Entry Date: 083199
                  Description: #3618-3618;3620-3669
                     Document:
                      Account: 120
                       Amount: -41086.49

Document Total   Batch Total   Journal Total   Ledger Total
          0.00          0.00            0.00          00.00


                      Enter Entry Number:       <

     This Option Will Allow You to View any Previous Entry
```

ENTERING GENERAL AND RECURRING JOURNAL ENTRIES

General Journal Entries

General journal entries are entered into the computer using the same screen as cash receipts and cash disbursements. The sequence of steps is as follows:

1. From the GENERAL LEDGER OPERATIONS GUIDE, select item:

    `(C) Add, Delete, or Change Journal Entries.`

    a. When the screen changes, select item:

    `(A) Add, Delete, or Change Journal Entries.`

    b. Again the screen changes, asking you which journal to select:

    `Select Journal: [Enter] C.`

    c. You are now ready to enter the journal entries. The screen looks like this:

Screen:	Comments:
Entry Number:	Assigned by the program
Entry Date:	Enter the last day of the month
Description:	Varies
Document:	Enter the journal number
Account:	Enter the appropriate account number
Amount:	Enter the amount of the entry

(1) Enter the debit side of the entry first.

(2) The credit side of the entry is made using the minus (−) sign.

The Journal Total and Ledger Total should *always* be zero at the end of a data entry session.

You may change any entry up until the time you perform the posting function from the General Ledger Operations Guide. After you have posted, you may still make changes to any line *except* the account number line. (To change an account number after posting, you must delete the original entry and reenter it.)

2. Once you have verified that the entries balance, go back to the GENERAL LEDGER OPERATIONS GUIDE by entering an **'R'—Return** *General Ledger Operations* on the screen after your last entry and **press the return key.**

3. Now perform the post function. From the GENERAL LEDGER OPERATIONS GUIDE select item:

    `(D) Post entries to Chart of Accounts.`

Recurring Journal Entries

The sequence of steps for entering Recurring Journal Entries is as follows:

1. From the GENERAL LEDGER OPERATIONS GUIDE, select item:

    `(C) Add, Delete, or Change Journal Entries.`

2. When the screen changes, select item:

    `(C) Generate Recurring Entries into Journal.`

3. You will then be asked to:

    `Select Recurring Entry File: [Enter] R.`

4. The program will next ask for the date of the recurring entries. This is the date that the accounting month ends. For example, August 31, 1999 would be entered as 083199.
5. When asked **Do You Want to Reverse Entries** enter **N** for no.
6. When asked to **Enter Source Document:** enter **R.**
7. Recurring entries will now be generated to the Recurring Journal Entry file.
8. Now perform the posting function. From the GENERAL LEDGER OPERATIONS GUIDE, select item:

    `(D) Post Entries to Chart of Accounts.`

EXITING THE GENERAL LEDGER PROGRAM

After you have completed each data entry session, there are certain procedures that must be followed when exiting the accounting program. The order of these procedures is important because, if they are not followed, it is possible to damage the data that is on the diskette.

1. The first step to signing off of the system is to return to the GENERAL LEDGER OPERATIONS GUIDE. This is usually done by entering an **'R'** and pressing the return key from whatever operation you are currently in. (There is another method of exiting the current menu: It is to simply press the return key. This method is available only in certain operations such as printing financial statements. In any event, the bottom of the screen will display instructions as to which method is required to exit the screen.)
2. Once you are back at the GENERAL LEDGER OPERATIONS GUIDE, select item **(R) Return to Master Selection Guide**. From the Master Selection Guide select item **(S) Sign Off**. A **C>** will appear on the screen indicating the sign-off procedure is complete. Backup copies of the data are made from the C> and are explained in Section 6, "Backup Procedures."

BACKUP PROCEDURES

Power failures, static electricity, magnets, equipment failure, operator error, damaged diskettes, and natural disasters can adversely affect the information contained on a diskette. For these reasons it is necessary to make frequent copies of the data contained on the hard disk. Data should be backed up after each data entry session. If the data entry session lasts more than a couple of hours, it may be necessary to back up more frequently.

Three 5¼-inch floppy diskettes are used for making backup. These diskettes have both permanent labels and temporary labels. The permanent labels identify the diskettes as backup diskettes for the general ledger system. The temporary labels have the date of the last backup session noted on them. When choosing which backup diskette to use, always use the diskette with the oldest date first.

When all transactions have been entered and verified for one month's activity, a fourth and fifth backup diskette should be made. Retain one of the diskettes for archival storage within the office. Label it with the month it contains backup for. The fifth diskette is for off-site storage. Label it as the off-site diskette and note the month it is for. As the name implies this diskette should be stored somewhere else other than at the office.

The procedures for backup are as follows:

1. From the **C>** prompt (see Section 5 [item 2], "Exiting the General Ledger Program") enter **A:** and press the return key.
2. Take out the **bring up** diskette from drive A.
3. Insert the oldest backup diskette into drive A and close the door.
4. At the **A>** enter: **copy d:*.abc** and press the return key.
5. After the message showing how many files were copied appears on the screen, remove the backup diskette and label it with the current date using a temporary label.
6. Replace the **bring up** diskette into drive A.
7. At the **A>** enter **C:** and press the return key.
8. Use the same procedure for making the archival and off-site storage diskettes. Ignore the instructions to insert the oldest backup diskette and place a newly formatted blank diskette in its place.

PROCEDURES FOR PRINTING REPORTS

The following procedures for printing reports cover only reports that are necessary to obtain monthly reports for ABC WATER COMPANY. The flexibility of the program and the number of reports covered in it does not permit a full explanation of each report or option in this document. Please refer to Chapter 5 of the General Ledger Instruction Manual for detailed instructions and examples of the screen layout if you are in doubt as to how to proceed.

JOURNALS

Journals such as Cash Receipts, Cash Disbursements, and the General Journal are printed on paper through option **(E)**

Print Journal Entries from the GENERAL LEDGER OPERATIONS GUIDE.

For a listing of all journals in your general ledger, refer to the General Ledger Data sheet printed out at conversion. To obtain a new listing of journals go through option **(A) Prepare Disk for New User** from the GENERAL LEDGER OPERATIONS GUIDE.

Screen **(E) Print Journal Entries** contains the following options:

(A) Print Entries in Chronological Sequence
(B) Print Entries in Document Sequence
(C) Print Entries in Date Sequence
(D) Print Recurring Entries
(E) Print Transaction Audit Entries
(F) Print Account Audit Entries

Most journals will be printed out using suboption **(A) Print Entries in Chronological Sequence**, which is located on the screen that comes after you have told the computer to print through option **(E).** However, you may want to use suboption **(B) Print Entries in Document Sequence** if you enter a group of document numbers (e.g., check numbers) in random order. Suboption **(B)** will put them in numerical sequence.

Suboption **(E) Print Transaction Audit Entries** will provide you with a listing of all entries that were changed or deleted during the period. Suboption **(F) Print Account Audit Entries** will provide you with a listing of all accounts that were deleted during the period.

THE GENERAL LEDGER

The general ledger is printed through option **(F) Print Accounts in Ledger Format** from the GENERAL LEDGER OPERATIONS GUIDE. This option allows you to either view an account or accounts to screen (or to view the entire general ledger) or to print out an account or accounts (or the entire general ledger) on paper.

TO PRINT THE GENERAL LEDGER

1. Select item **(F) Print Accounts in Ledger Format** from the GENERAL LEDGER OPERATIONS GUIDE.

2. When the screen changes, enter the date of the general ledger to be printed. Press the return key.

3. At the next screen, enter the range of accounts. For a full general ledger, this will be all accounts, so press the return key. (For selected accounts, you would put a range of numbers. For example, if you wanted all cash accounts from account number 120 to account number 121.2, you would enter '120-121.2.')

4. Next you will be asked for department number to print. Press the return key for all departments.

5. If you wish to omit accounts that have zero balances (and which have not had any activity since they were set up), answer **'Y'** for yes when asked to print accounts with activity only at the next screen.

6. When asked for the period to print, enter **'Y'** for year-to-date if you wish to obtain a listing of the transactions entered since the date of conversion or from the beginning of the year. Otherwise, select **'R'** for a range of dates. You will then be requested to enter the dates you wish the printout to show. For example, to print the month of October you would enter '100199-103199.'

7. The last step is to select whether you want to view the account or accounts to screen or to print them to paper. Your options are:

   a. To view on the screen, select: **'D' for display.**
   b. To print to paper, select: **'P' for printer.**

TRIAL BALANCE WORKSHEET

This worksheet may be used to make adjustments to the accounts prior to entering the adjustments into the computer. To print or view a Trial Balance Worksheet, use option **(G) Print Trial Balance Worksheet** from the GENERAL LEDGER OPERATIONS GUIDE.

FINANCIAL STATEMENTS

From the GENERAL LEDGER OPERATIONS GUIDE, select:

```
(L) Print Standard Style Financial
    Statements.
```

For a listing of all financial statement formats in your general ledger, refer to the List of Financial Statement Formats printed out at conversion. To obtain a new listing of formats, go through option **(I) Add or Change a Financial Statement Format** from the GENERAL LEDGER OPERATIONS GUIDE.

TO PRINT THE BALANCE SHEET: LONG FORM

From the GENERAL LEDGER OPERATIONS GUIDE, select:

```
(L) Print Standard Style Financial
    Statements.
```

1. Select print format: `A.`
2. Enter the date of the report. Press the return key.
3. Enter the report date only if you wish to override the date standard title that has been set up in the system. Otherwise press the return key.
4. Enter the report date only if you wish to override the date that was put in through #2 above. Otherwise press the return key.
5. When asked to enter the footnote, press the return key unless you wish to add a footnote. (There is no standard footnote set up for ABC WATER COMPANY. This feature is useful if you are running a trial statement. It can be used to keep track of the number of runs and thereby avoid confusion as to which is the most current run. You may also find some other uses for it. Experimenting with this and other features of the program will help you find other ways to use the software.)

6. Answer **'N'** for no when asked if you want to print a chart of accounts.

7. Answer **'Y'** for yes when asked if you want to print accounts with balances only. This will keep your balance sheet clean by not printing accounts with zero balances (which have not previously had activity in them).

8. Press the return key when asked for which department to print.

9. Enter **'Y'** for year-to-date when asked to select the period to print.

10. Enter **'P'** for printer when asked to select print option. To view on the screen, select **'D'** for display.

NOTE: The procedure to print the Balance Sheet: Short Form is the same as described above except that item 1 will be: Select print format: C.

TO PRINT THE STATEMENT OF EARNINGS

From the GENERAL LEDGER OPERATIONS GUIDE, select:

```
(L) Print Standard Style Financial
    Statements.
```

1. Select print format: B.
2. Enter the date of the report. Press the return key.
3. Enter the report title only if you wish to override the date standard title that has been set up in the system. Otherwise press the return key.
4. Enter the report date only if you wish to override the date that was put in through #2 above. Otherwise press the return key.
5. When asked to enter the footnote, press the return key unless you wish to add a footnote. (There is no standard footnote set up for ABC WATER COMPANY. This feature is useful if you are running a trial statement. It can be used to keep track of the number of runs and thereby avoid confusion as to which is the most current run. You may also find some other uses for it.

Experimenting with this and other features of the program will help you find other ways to use the software.)

6. Answer **'N'** for no when asked if you want to print a chart of accounts.

7. Answer **'Y'** for yes when asked if you want to print accounts with balances only. This will keep your income statement clean by not printing accounts with zero balances (which have not previously had activity in them).

8. Press the return key when asked for which department to print.

9. Enter **'C'** for current period when asked to select the period to print.

10. Enter **'P'** for printer when asked to select print option. To view on the screen, select **'D'** for display.

TO PRINT THE CHART OF ACCOUNTS

From the GENERAL LEDGER OPERATIONS GUIDE, select:

```
(L) Print Standard Style Financial
    Statements.
```

1. Select print format: `D`.

2. Enter the date of the report. Press the return key.

3. Enter the report title only if you wish to override the standard title that has been set up in the system. Otherwise press the return key.

4. Enter the report date only if you wish to override the date that was put in through #2 above. Otherwise press the return key.

5. When asked to enter the footnote, press the return key unless you wish to add a footnote. (There is no standard footnote set up for ABC WATER COMPANY. This feature is useful if you are running a trial chart of accounts. It can be used to keep track of the number of runs and thereby avoid confusion as to which is the most current run. You may also find some other uses for it. Experimenting with this and other features of the program will help you find other ways to use the software.)

6. Answer **'Y'** for yes when asked if you want to print a chart of accounts.

7. Press the return key when asked for department to print.

8. Enter **'P'** for printer when asked to select print option. To view on the screen, select **'D'** for display.

TO PRINT THE COMPARATIVE BALANCE SHEET: LONG FORM

From the GENERAL LEDGER OPERATIONS GUIDE, select:

```
(K) Print Budget Style Financial
    Statements.
```

1. Select print format: **A**.

2. Enter the date of the report. Press the return key.

3. Enter the report title only if you wish to override the standard title that has been set up in the system. Otherwise press the return key.

4. Enter the report date only if you wish to override the date that was put in through #2 above. Otherwise press the return key.

5. When asked to enter the footnote press the return key unless you wish to add a footnote. (There is no standard footnote set up for ABC WATER COMPANY. This feature is useful if you are running a trial statement. It can be used to keep track of the number of runs and thereby avoid confusion as to which is the most current run. You may also find some other uses for it. Experimenting with this and other features of the program will help you find other ways to use the software.)

6. Press the return key when asked for which department to print.

7. Answer **'Y'** for yes when asked if you want to print accounts with balances only. This will keep your balance sheet clean by not printing accounts with zero balances (which have not previously had activity in them).

8. Enter **'Y'** for year-to-date when asked to select the period to print.

9. When asked for a range of budgets, enter the (calendar) number of the month you are printing the comparatives for. For

example, if you were printing comparatives for the month of August, the range would be '8-8.'

10. Enter **'P'** for printer when asked to select print option. To view on the screen, select **'D'** for display.

NOTE: The procedure to print the Comparative Balance Sheet: Short Form is the same as described above except that item 1 will be: Select print format: C. To print the Comparative Income Statement item 1 will be: Select print format: B.

PERFORMING THE ANNUAL CLOSING

The annual closing is performed at the end of the year only after the entries have been verified, the backup copies have been made, and the reports have been printed.

1. From the GENERAL LEDGER OPERATIONS GUIDE, select option:

    `(N) Update Balances or Delete Accounts.`

2. When the screen changes, select:

    `(B) Update Current Journal Entries.`

3. Next you are asked to enter the period ending date. This will be the date of the annual closing. For example, if you are closing for the year ended December 31, 1999, the date would be 123199.
4. You will then be asked to enter the range of accounts to close and the account to close them into. Enter the following:
    a. For the range of accounts, enter: **500-1000;**
    b. For the account to close them into, enter: **330.271.**
5. Next the program will ask:

    `Add Entries into a Budget?`

    Answer this question with a **'Y'** for yes.
6. Finally you will be asked:

    `Do You Desire to Continue?`

    Answer this question with a **'Y'** for yes.
7. The computer will now update the accounts. All income and expense accounts will be cleared to show a zero balance; the retained earnings account will be updated with the net profit (loss) accumulated at the end of the year.

APPENDIX G
SAMPLE SCREENS AND REPORTS

FIGURE G.1 Sample Data Entry Screens for Accounts Receivable Customer Setup. Courtesy of The Business Library.

```
11/13/83                  A / R   C U S T O M E R   F I L E
                                Knight & Company, CPAs

CUSTOMER NUMBER            [        ]
       1. Name             [                              ]
       2.                  [                              ]
       3. STREET           [                              ]
       4.                  [                              ]
       5. CITY             [             ]  6. STATE  [  ]  7. ZIP [        ]
       8. PHONE            [           ]
 9. RESALE (Y/N)           [ ]
10. TAX CODES              [      ]
11. BILLING CODE           [   ]
12. SALESMAN NUMBER        [    ]
13. CREDIT LIMIT           [           ]
14. CREDIT CONTACT         [              ]
15. FINANCE CHARGE (Y/N) [ ]                                S A L E S
16. CYCLE (M/W/N)          [ ]
17. CASH ON ACCOUNT        [           ]   20. CURRENT MONTH [             ]
18. CLASSIFICATION         [      ]        21. YEAR TO DATE  [             ]
19. HISTORY PAYMENT CODE [  ]              22. LAST YEAR     [             ]

OPTIONS:   F1) ADD   F2)  CHANGE  F3) DELETE  F4) INQUIRE   F5) LIST  F6) LOG
SELECT OPTION DESIRED BY PRESSING CORRESPONDING FUNCTION KEY
ARCUST(2.0) Publisher: Software Libraries Inc.
(C)1982 DynaMicro Software Corp.
```

Screen 1: This is how the screen looks initially when this function is requested by the operator.

```
11/13/83                 A / R   C U S T O M E R   F I L E              * ADD *
                              Knight & Company, CPAs

CUSTOMER NUMBER          [12345678]
      1. NAME            [ABC Imports, Limited          ]
      2.                 [                              ]
      3. STREET          [1234 Anystreet                ]
      4.                 [                              ]
      5. CITY            [San Francisco  ]   6. STATE  [CA]   7. ZIP [99999    ]
      8. PHONE           [(123)456-7890]
 9. RESALE (Y/N)         [N]
10. TAX CODES            [     ]
11. BILLING CODE         [  ]
12. SALESMAN NUMBER      [01 ]
13. CREDIT LIMIT         [     50,000.00]
14. CREDIT CONTACT       [Joe Lee        ]
15. FINANCE CHARGE (Y/N) [Y]                                   S A L E S
16. CYCLE (M/W/N)        [M]
17. CASH ON ACCOUNT      [          0.00]   20. CURRENT MONTH [    10,000.00]
18. CLASSIFICATION       [A   ]             21. YEAR TO DATE  [    25,000.00]
19. HISTORY PAYMENT CODE [  ]               22. LAST YEAR     [   100,000.00]

OPTIONS:  F1) ACCEPT  F2) CHANGE  F4) REJECT
SELECT OPTION DESIRED BY PRESSING CORRESPONDING FUNCTION KEY
ARCUST(2.0) Publisher: Software Libraries Inc.
(C)1982 DynaMicro Software Corp.
```

Screen 2: The same screen as shown above, but after customer information has been entered. The computer is now waiting for the operator to select one of the options (F1, F2, or F4).

FIGURE G.1 (con.)

FIGURE G.2 Same Setup Screens for Accounts Payable. Courtesy of The Business Library.

```
11/13/83   A / P   C O N T R O L  I N F O  D E F I N I T I O N

 1. COMPANY NUMBER               [  ]
 2. PROCESSING DATE              [        ]
 3. CURRENT ACCOUNTING PERIOD    [  ]
 4. LAST ACCOUNTING PERIOD       [  ]
 5. DISCOUNT DATE                [        ]
 6. A/P ACCOUNT 1                [            ]
 7. A/P ACCOUNT 2                [            ]
 8. A/P ACCOUNT 3                [            ]
 9. A/P ACCOUNT 4                [            ]
10. CASH ACCOUNT 1               [            ]
11. CASH ACCOUNT 2               [            ]
12. CASH ACCOUNT 3               [            ]
13. CASH ACCOUNT 4               [            ]
14. DISC ACCOUNT                 [            ]
15. G/L INSTALL                  [ ]
16. I/C INSTALL                  [ ]
17. P/O INSTALL                  [ ]
18. BATCH REFERENCE              [      ]

ENTER COMPANY NUMBER AND PRESS ENTER
APCTRL(2.0) Publisher: Software Libraries Inc.
(C)1982 DynaMicro Software Corp.
```

Screen 1: This is how the screen looks initially when this function is requested by the operator.

```
11/13/83   A / P   C O N T R O L   I N F O   D E F I N I T I O N

  1. COMPANY NUMBER                [01]               Knight & Company, CPAs
  2. PROCESSING DATE               [11/30/83]
  3. CURRENT ACCOUNTING PERIOD     [11]
  4. LAST ACCOUNTING PERIOD        [10]
  5. DISCOUNT DATE                 [11/15/83]
  6. A/P ACCOUNT 1                 [2100-00-00]
  7. A/P ACCOUNT 2                 [2100-00-01]
  8. A/P ACCOUNT 3                 [2100-00-02]
  9. A/P ACCOUNT 4                 [2100-00-03]
 10. CASH ACCOUNT 1                [1100-00-00]
 11. CASH ACCOUNT 2                [1100-00-01]
 12. CASH ACCOUNT 3                [1100-00-02]
 13. CASH ACCOUNT 4                [1100-00-03]
 14. DISC ACCOUNT                  [7110-00-00]
 15. G/L INSTALL                   [N]
 16. I/C INSTALL                   [N]
 17. P/O INSTALL                   [N]
 18. BATCH REFERENCE               [0000]

OPTIONS:  F1) ACCEPT  F2) CHANGE  F4) REJECT
SELECT OPTION DESIRED BY PRESSING CORRESPONDING FUNCTION KEY
APCTRL(2.0) Publisher: Software Libraries Inc.
(C)1982 DynaMicro Software Corp.
```

Screen 2: The same screen as shown above, but after the operator has entered the company's setup information.

FIGURE G.2 (con.)

FIGURE G.3 Sample Inquiry Screens: Accounts Payable for Recalling Data on One Vendor. Courtesy of The Business Library.

```
11/13/83          VENDOR MASTER FILE MAINTENANCE / INQUIRY
                            Knight & Company, CPAs

   VENDOR NUMBER       [       ]

 1. NAME               [                             ]
 2. SHORT NAME         [              ]
 3. ADDRESS LINE I     [                             ]
 4. ADDRESS LINE II    [                             ]
 5. CITY               [              ]
 6. STATE              [  ]
 7. ZIP                [         ]
 8. PHONE              [            ]
 9. CONTACT            [              ]
10. CLASSIFICATION     [   ]
11. DATE ACCOUNT OPENED [      ]
12. LAST PURCHASE DATE [      ]
13. VENDOR RATING      [  ]
14. MTD PURCHASES      [         ]
15. YTD PURCHASES      [         ]
16. LAST YEAR PURCHASES [         ]

OPTIONS: F1) ADD  F2) CHANGE  F3) DELETE F4) INQUIRE  F5) LIST  F6) LOG
SELECT OPTION DESIRED BY PRESSING CORRESPONDING FUNCTION KEY
APVEND(2.0B) Publisher: Software Libraries Inc.
(C)1982 DynaMicro Software Corp.
```

Screen 1: Prior to entry of vendor number.

```
11/13/83          VENDOR MASTER FILE MAINTENANCE / INQUIRY  * INQUIRE *
                              Knight & Company, CPAs

   VENDOR NUMBER         [1234567]

 1. NAME                 [XYZ Exports, Unlimited          ]
 2. SHORT NAME           [XYZ Exports    ]
 3. ADDRESS LINE I       [1234 Anystreet                  ]
 4. ADDRESS LINE II      [                                ]
 5. CITY                 [San Francisco  ]
 6. STATE                [CA]
 7. ZIP                  [99999     ]
 8. PHONE                [(123)456-7890]
 9. CONTACT              [Joe Lee        ]
10. CLASSIFICATION       [A  ]
11. DATE ACCOUNT OPENED  [01/01/75]
12. LAST PURCHASE DATE   [11/01/83]
13. VENDOR RATING        [ 1]
14. MTD PURCHASES        [ 10,000.00]
15. YTD PURCHASES        [ 25,000.00]
16. LAST YEAR PURCHASES  [100,000.00]

PRESS ANY KEY TO CONTINUE
APVEND(2.0B) Publisher: Software Libraries Inc.
(C)1982 DynaMicro Software Corp.
```

Screen 2: After entering vendor number, all other information is called to the screen.

FIGURE G.3 (con.)

FIGURE G.4. Sample Menu Screen for telling the accounts payable system how to generate checks for paying vendors. Courtesy of The Business Library.

```
11/13/83            P A Y M E N T   S E L E C T I O N
                            Knight & Company, CPAs

         ACCOUNTINGPERIOD:  11         PROCESSING DATE: 11/30/83

1. ALL OPEN INVOICES
2. ALL DUE BY 'MM/DD/YY'
3. ALL WITH DISCOUNT ELIGIBLE BY 'MM/DD/YY'
4. ALL OPEN FOR VENDOR
5. SELECTIVE INVOICE
6. PARTIAL PAYMENT
7. CANCEL PAYMENT
8. PUT HOLD / RELEASE FOR PAYMENT
9. PRINT PAYMENT SELECTION REGISTER
10. CLEAR PAYMENT SELECTION REGISTER


SELECTION [  ]

ENTER SELECTION DESIRED AND PRESS ENTER
APPSEL(2.0) Publisher: Software Libraries Inc.
(C)1982 DynaMicro Software Corp.
```

FIGURE G.5 A Typical Chart of Accounts.

SAMPLE CORPORATION CHART OF ACCOUNTS
APRIL 30, 1999

Assets

1010.0000	Cash-general account
1011.0000	Cash-savings
1020.0000	Petty cash
1030.0000	Short-term investments
1110.0000	Accounts receivable-trade
1111.0000	Accounts receivable-other
1120.0000	Deposits on future purchases
1200.0000	Inventory-raw materials
1210.0000	Inventory-finished goods
1300.0000	Prepaid expense
1302.0000	Deferred interest
1401.0000	Office furniture and fixtures
1402.0000	Automotive equipment
1403.0000	Capital containers
1500.0000	Accumulated depreciation
1575.0000	Deferred tax benefit
1600.0000	Organization costs
1605.0000	Sales tax bond

Liabilities

2010.0000	Loan from stockholder
2015.0000	Short-term bank loan
2016.0000	Contracts payable
2020.0000	Accounts payable-trade
2021.0000	Accounts payable-other
2030.0000	Customer deposits
2035.0000	Current maturities
2040.0000	Sales tax payable
2050.0000	Federal income tax withheld
2051.0000	FICA tax withheld
2052.0000	State income tax withheld

FIGURE G.5 A Typical Chart of Accounts (con.)

SAMPLE CORPORATION CHART OF ACCOUNTS
APRIL 30, 1999

Liabilities

2053.0000	SDI tax withheld
2110.0000	Accrued payroll
2120.0000	Other accrued expenses
2130.0000	Income taxes payable
2140.0000	Other accrued expenses
2200.0000	Contracts payable

Stockholders' Equity

3010.0000	Common stock issued
3030.0000	Retained earnings

Income

4020.0000	Sales-taxable
4021.0000	Sales-nontaxable
4022.0000	Discounts and allowances

Cost of Goods Sold

5010.0000	Purchases
5011.0000	Freight
5012.0000	Inventory adjustment
5013.0000	Laboratory
5020.0000	Depreciation-capital container

Selling Expenses

6010.0000	Salaries
6140.0000	Dues and subcriptions
6230.0000	Delivery
6240.0000	Advertising
6250.0000	Bad debts
6260.0000	Miscellaneous
6270.0000	Other selling expenses

FIGURE G.5 A Typical Chart of Accounts (con.)

SAMPLE CORPORATION CHART OF ACCOUNTS
APRIL 30, 1999

General and Administrative

7010.0000	Officers' salaries
7020.0000	Office salaries
7090.0000	Telephone
7100.0000	Insurance
7120.0000	Office supplies and expense
7130.0000	Travel and entertainment
7131.0000	Auto
7140.0000	Dues and subscriptions
7150.0000	Payroll tax expense
7160.0000	Contributions
7180.0000	Rent
7190.0000	Depreciation and amortization
7250.0000	Legal and accounting
7260.0000	Employee benefits
7280.0000	Miscellaneous

Other Income and Expense

8010.0000	Interest expense
8015.0000	Interest income
8020.0000	Provision for taxes
8025.0000	Tax benefit-net operating loss

FIGURE G.6 A Typical Trial Balance.

SAMPLE CORPORATION
WORKING TRIAL BALANCE
04-30-99

Account #	Account Title	Debit Balance	Credit Balance	Entries	New Balance
1010	Cash-general account	51,895.74			
1011	Cash-savings	368.03			
1020	Petty cash	200.00			
1030	Short-term investments	118,000.00			
1110	Accounts receivable-trade	684,852.81			
1111	Accounts receivable-other	454.32			
1120	Deposits on future purchase	161,582.64			
1200	Inventory—raw materials	2,383.00			
1210	Inventory—finished goods	16,010.00			
1300	Prepaid expense	348.00			
1302	Deferred interest	0.00			
1401	Office furniture and fixtures	6,036.92			
1402	Automotive equipment	18,340.38			
1403	Capital containers	7,758.00			
1500	Accumulated depreciation		14,977.00		
1575	Deferred tax benefit	1,200.00			
1600	Organization costs	561.05			
1605	Sales tax bond	800.00			
2010	Loan from stockholder		65,724.09		
2015	Short-term bank loan		20,000.00		
2016	Contracts payable	0.00			
2020	Accounts payable—trade		144,974.52		
2021	Accounts payable—other	0.00			
2030	Customer deposits		173,792.50		
2035	Current maturities		4,692.00		
2040	Sales tax payable		976.88		
2050	Federal income tax withheld	0.00			
2051	FICA tax withheld		594.17		
2052	State income tax withheld		743.90		
2053	SDI tax withheld		174.17		
2110	Accrued payroll		32,635.00		

FIGURE G.6 A Typical Trial Balance. (con.)

SAMPLE CORPORATION
WORKING TRIAL BALANCE
04-30-99

Account #	Account Title	Debit Balance	Credit Balance	Entries	New Balance
2120	Other accrued expenses		8,009.66		
2130	Income taxes payable		4,200.00		
2200	Contracts payable		7,917.64		
3010	Common stock issued		50,000.00		
3030	Retained earnings		64,750.95		
4020	Sales—taxable		843,698.01		
4021	Sales—nontaxable		1,004,275.78		
4022	Discounts and allowances	11,037.92			
5010	Purchases	1,208,972.41			
5011	Freight	107.70			
5012	Inventory adjustment		23,219.00		
5013	Laboratory	4,456.50			
5020	Depreciation—capital containers	3,198.00			
6010	Salaries	3,385.00			
6140	Dues and subscriptions	1,197.00			
6230	Delivery	18,723.02			
6240	Advertising	1,095.00			
6250	Bad debts	4,838.30			
6260	Miscellaneous	535.12			
6270	Other selling expenses	6,006.84			
7010	Officers' salaries	65,000.00			
7020	Office salaries	5,384.61			
7090	Telephone	6,017.94			
7100	Insurance	232.00			
7120	Office supplies and expense	4,175.93			
7130	Travel and entertainment	9,145.65			
7131	Auto	5,160.12			
7140	Dues and subscriptions	34.30			
7150	Payroll tax expense	4,664.28			
7160	Contributions	30.00			
7180	Rent	2,640.00			

FIGURE G.6 A Typical Trial Balance. (con.)

SAMPLE CORPORATION
WORKING TRIAL BALANCE
04-30-99

Account #	Account Title	Debit Balance	Credit Balance	Entries	New Balance
7190	Depreciation and amortization	12,695.00		______	______
7250	Legal and accounting	15,470.32		______	______
7260	Employee benefits	3,311.12		______	______
7280	Miscellaneous	1,128.19		______	______
8010	Interest expense	11,750.74		______	______
8015	Interest income		19,028.63	______	______
8020	Provision for taxes	4,300.00		______	______
8025	Tax benefit—net operating loss		1,100.00	______	______
	Total Debit Balance	$2,485,483.90			
	Total Credit Balance	-2,485,483.90			
	Total Difference	$0.00			

FIGURE G.7. A Typical General Ledger (partial).

SAMPLE CORPORATION
GENERAL LEDGER
04-30-99

Entry	Date	Description	Document	J1	Debits	Credits	Balance
(1120)		*Deposits on future purchases*					
	033199	BALANCE FORWARD					41495.22
16	043099	April summary	CRS	A		976.20	
31	043099	April summary	CDS	B	161185.90		
51	043099	4-30-99 accrual	GJ 1	C		2274.91	
84	043099	Reclassify check 739	GJ 9	C		976.26	
86	043099	Order filled	GJ 10	C		37847.31	
119	043099	Adjust to recon.	GJ 24	C	976.20		
	TOTALS	Deposits on future purchases			162162.10	42074.68	$161582.64

FIGURE G.7 A Typical General Ledger (partial). (con.)

SAMPLE CORPORATION
GENERAL LEDGER
04-30-99

Entry	Date	Description	Document	J1	Debits	Credits	Balance
(1200)		*Inventory-raw materials*					
	033199	BALANCE FORWARD					0.00
54	043099	Trans. raw materials	GJ 3	C	2383.00		
	TOTALS	Inventory-raw materials			2383.00	0.00	$2383.00
(1210)		*Inventory-finished goods*					
	033199	BALANCE FORWARD					20283.37
53	043099	Inventory adjustment	GJ 2	C		1890.37	
55	043099	Trans. raw materials	GJ 3	C		2383.00	
	TOTALS	Inventory—finished goods			0.00	4273.37	$16010.00
(1300)		*Prepaid expense*					
	033199	BALANCE FORWARD					1160.00
88	043099	Amortization	GJ 11	C		812.00	
	TOTALS	Prepaid expense			0.00	812.00	$348.00
(1302)		*Deferred interest*					
	033199	BALANCE FORWARD					7918.02
97	043099	Interest amortization	GJ 15	C		587.17	
128	043099	Deferred interest	RA a	R		7330.85	
	TOTALS	Deferred interest			0.00	7918.02	$0.00
(1401)		*Office furniture and fixtures*					
	033199	BALANCE FORWARD					1763.88
32	043099	April summary	CDS	B	953.18		
57	043099	Reverse 3-31-99 AP	GJ 4	C		590.24	
67	043099	Record 4-30-99 AP	GJ 5	C	2870.17		
89	043099	Reclass. cap. equip.	GJ 12	C	1039.93		
	TOTALS	Office furniture and fixtures			4863.28	590.24	$6036.92

FIGURE G.8 A Typical Income Statement.

SAMPLE CORPORATION
STATEMENT OF EARNINGS
April 30, 1999

INCOME FROM OPERATIONS:				
Net sales	1,836,935.87	100.0		
Cost of good sold	1,193,515.61	65.0		
GROSS MARGIN			643,420.26	35.0
EXPENSES:				
Selling expenses	35,780.28	1.9		
Officers' salaries	65,000.00	3.5		
Office salaries	5,384.61	0.3		
Telephone	6,017.94	0.3		
Insurance	232.00	0.0		
Office supplies and expense	4,175.93	0.2		
Travel and entertainment	9,145.65	0.5		
Auto	5,160.12	0.3		
Dues and subscriptions	34.30	0.0		
Payroll tax expense	4,664.28	0.3		
Contributions	30.00	0.0		
Rent	2,640.00	0.1		
Depreciation and amortization	12,695.00	0.7		
Legal and accounting	15,470.32	0.8		
Employee benefits	3,311.12	0.2		
Miscellaneous	1,128.19	0.1		
			170,869.74	9.3
Operating income			472,550.52	25.7
OTHER INCOME —EXPENSE:				
Interest expense	11,750.74	0.6		
Interest income	19,028.63	1.0		
			7,277.89	0.4
NET EARNINGS BEFORE TAX			479,828.41	26.1

FIGURE G.8 A Typical Income Statement. (con.)

SAMPLE CORPORATION
STATEMENT OF EARNINGS
April 30, 1999

TAXES ON INCOME:				
Provision for taxes	4,300.00	0.2		
			4,300.00	0.2
NET EARNINGS BEFORE NOL			475,528.41	25.9
TAX BENEFIT FROM NOL				
Tax benefit—net operating loss	1,100.00	0.1		
			1,100.00	0.1
NET EARNINGS			$476,628.41	25.9

FIGURE G.9 A Typical Balance Sheet.

SAMPLE CORPORATION
BALANCE SHEET
APRIL 30, 1999

Assets

CURRENT ASSETS:		
Cash and cash equivalents	52,463.77	
Short-term investments	118,000.00	
Accounts receivable-trade	684,852.81	
Accounts receivable-other	454.32	
Deposits on future purchases	161,582.64	
Inventory-raw materials	2,383.00	
Inventory-finished goods	16,010.00	
Prepaid expense	348.00	
TOTAL CURRENT ASSETS		1,036,094.54

FIGURE G.9 A Typical Balance Sheet. (con.)

SAMPLE CORPORATION
BALANCE SHEET
APRIL 30, 1999

Assets

PROPERTY AND EQUIPMENT:		
Office furniture and fixtures	6,036.92	
Automotive equipment	18,340.38	
Capital containers	7,758.00	
		32,135.30
Less:		
Accumulated depreciation	14,977.00	
		14,977.00
TOTAL PROPERTY & EQUIPMENT		17,158.30
DEFERRED TAX BENEFIT:		
Deferred tax benefit	1,200.00	
		1,200.00
ORGANIZATION COSTS, net:		
Organization costs	561.05	
		561.05
OTHER ASSETS:		
Sales tax bond	800.00	
		800.00
		$1,055,813.89

FIGURE G.9 A Typical Balance Sheet. (con.)

SAMPLE CORPORATION
BALANCE SHEET
APRIL 30, 1999

Liabilities and Equity

CURRENT LIABILITIES:		
Loan from stockholder	65,724.09	
Short-term bank loan	20,000.00	
Accounts payable-trade	144,974.52	
Customer deposits	173,792.50	
Current maturities	4,692.00	
Sales tax payable	976.88	
Payroll taxes withheld	1,512.24	
Accrued expenses	40,644.66	
Income taxes payable	4,200.00	
TOTAL CURRENT LIABILITIES		456,516.89
LONG-TERM DEBT, net:		
Contracts payable	7,917.64	
		7,917.64
STOCKHOLDERS' EQUITY:		
Common stock issued	50,000.00	
Retained earnings	64,750.95	
Current earnings	476,628.41	
		591,379.36
		$1,055,813.89

GLOSSARY

Account number. A number assigned to the accumulation of a specific category of financial transactions. The account number may be for a general ledger account, for a customer, or for a vendor.

Accounting. The theory and practice of maintaining the financial records of a business and reporting that data in a standardized way.

Accounting security. The area of assuring that the accounting system is indeed reporting accurately and correctly the financial history of the business.

Accounts. The categories that the business has determined to be important for management decision making or government-reporting requirements. The accounts are standardly divided into five major types: assets, liabilities, equity, income, and expense.

Accounts payable. That part of the accounting system pertaining to amounts owed to outside vendors for the purchase of goods or services on credit. Also referred to as payables or AP.

Accounts receivable. That part of the accounting system pertaining to amounts owed to the business from credit sales. Also referred to as receivables or AR.

Adjusting journal entries. Transaction entries that are made by accountants to reflect internal adjustments (e.g., when the physical inventory count doesn't match the book value) or to reflect accrued transactions (e.g., when one-twelfth of the annual insurance payment is entered into the books each month). Also called AJEs.

Aged payables report. Report showing the status of each vendor's outstanding invoices, grouped into three or four date ranges (and thus by their age). This information is very useful for deciding what invoices to pay at any point in time. Also used for projections of cash requirements.

Aged receivables report. Report showing how much each customer owes, with the amounts grouped into three or four date ranges (and thus by their age). This information is useful for tracking the payment performance of customers and for determining the type of actions necessary to collect your receivables. Also used for projections of cash requirements.

Amortization. The reduction of the value of an intangible asset over time in accordance with certain established guidelines.

Audit trails. Procedures which allow the tracing of a transaction entry through the system (e.g., from the original documents to the various reported amounts).

Backup. The process of making duplicate copies of important data, so that if something happens to the original copy in the computer, the backup copies can be utilized. Without such backup copies, recovery can be difficult or even impossible.

Balance sheet. Report summarizing the status of the asset, liability, and equity accounts at a specified point in time. The amount of detail that is shown on this report can vary, depending on the desires of the business management and the flexibility of the accounting system.

Bookkeeping. The practice of entering information into an established accounting system.

Byte. A unit of information within a computer. One byte often represents one letter or number.

Cash disbursement. A payment made by a business in the form of currency, check, money order, or bank transfer.

Cash receipts. A payment received in the form of currency, check, money order, or bank transfer.

Cash requirements report. Any report showing the amounts of cash needed by the business at various times in order to pay certain bills. These reports vary greatly in the different accounting software packages.

Chart of accounts. A listing of the general ledger accounts in numerical order and divided into five categories: assets, liabilities and capital, income, and expenses. The list includes each account number followed by a description of that account.

Closing. In accounting this means the process of putting the books in order at the end of an accounting period, entering the usual closing entries, using the trial balance worksheet to verify that the system is in balance, and then producing the financial statements for that period. Many accounting programs use this term in confusing ways. For example, it may refer to an operation where the computer erases all transaction details, retaining only the net amount brought forward to start the next period with.

Control accounts. Accounts in the general ledger that accumulate the transactions for a specific subledger or category. For example, a business will usually have one or more accounts receivable control accounts in its general ledger; summary journal entries are made from the accounts receivable journal(s) into the accounts receivable control account(s).

Conversion process. The process of changing from one type of accounting system to another, such as from a manual accounting system to a computerized accounting system.

CPA. Stands for Certified Public Accountant. This title indicates an accountant who has earned a state license through certain accounting courses and exams and a long internship working for an established CPA firm.

Cursor. A small marker on the computer's display screen. Its purpose is to show where the next entry will begin.

Customer ledger. The transaction ledger that contains all of the transaction entries pertaining to your customers.

Data diskette. A floppy diskette that is used to store information as it is entered into the accounting system.

Data input form. The document from which data is read and entered into the computer. Sometimes it is more efficient to make up a special form that follows the format of the computer's input screen, rather than using the original documents directly.

Data security. The area of assuring that the data stored within the computer system remains accurate uncorrupted by the hardware or software or by some external electrical event.

Default entries. An entry that is offered by the computer system to the data entry operator. If the default is the desired date, account number, and so on, then it saves typing it in; if the default is not correct, the correct data can be entered in its place.

Depreciation. The reduction of the value of a fixed asset over time in accordance with certain established guidelines.

Diskette drive. A computer component which reads and writes to floppy diskettes.

Documentation. Any instructional, reference, and/or maintenance manual for the product involved.

Dot matrix printer. A printer that constructs each character from a pattern of dots; this type of printer typically prints much faster than a letter quality printer, but the characters are not quite as well-formed.

Dual floppy system. A computer system that uses two floppy diskette drives for storage of programs and data. By using two drives, the system can easily copy from one diskette to another. It also gives you the capability of using one drive for the computer program (the software you buy at the computer store) and the second drive for the data (such as the accounting records of your company).

End-of-Period Processing. Accounting systems generally divide the year into several accounting periods, usually by month or by quarter. At the end of each accounting period the accountants make their adjusting entries and bring the books up-to-date; then they can generate financial statements.

Exception report. Rather than listing all of the information available, this type of report just lists the desired information. For example, if you are interested in which customers have been paying late, you want a report which lists only those customers. The alternative is to get a listing of all customers and their payment histories, then go through that list and find the ones which paid late.

Files. Information stored on diskettes and hard disks is organized into files, similar to the way information in a filing cabinet is organized into manila file folders. Each file must have a name (its "label") and can contain different types and amounts of data.

Financial transaction. A financial transaction is any event that causes an entry to be made into the accounting records.

Floppy diskette. A flexible disk in a plastic shield. A magnetic coating on the disk can retain information; a computer's diskette drives can write information onto a diskette, read that information any number of times, and erase it. A typical floppy diskette can hold approximately 180 pages of double spaced text (360 thousand bytes).

Formatting. A new floppy diskette is completely empty of information. Before computer programs can use such a diskette, the computer's operating system must be used to put a pattern of addresses onto the diskette. This operation is called formatting the diskette, and it allows programs to locate different storage locations on the diskette.

Future Payments Due Report. This report tells you how much money is due to you (or from you, in accounts payable) during various time intervals in the future, based on the invoices you have entered into the computer and their due dates.

General ledger. A summarized record of all of a business' financial transactions. Also the name of the software module that produces the general ledger and the financial statements; also called the GL module.

Hard disk. A storage device similar to a floppy diskette and drive. It has a thick hard disk built into the drive (it cannot be removed); because the disk is fixed, it can hold many times as much data and can transfer it much faster than the floppy diskette.

Hardware. The actual machinery that makes up a computer. The machinery cannot do anything without being told what to do by the programs that are loaded into it.

Income statement. One of the standard financial statements. The Income Statement reports the net transactions into and out of your income and expense accounts over a specified time interval and gives the net income or loss for the period.

Journal. A record of individual transactions. Also known as books of original entry.

Ledger. A record that contains a list of accounts and the transaction entries and balance of those accounts.

Letter quality printer. A printer that forms characters like a typewriter; a hammer mechanism strikes a letter-shaped anvil to print each letter. This type of printer is relatively slow, but the letters formed are equal in quality to a typewriter's letters.

Local area network. This is a way to take several microcomputers and link them together to communicate, share data storage, and such equipment as printers. To implement a network you would have to install some electronic hardware into each microcomputer, connect them with cables, and load in some special networking software.

Maintenance contract. This is a contract between a computer owner and a computer repair facility. Usually there is a fixed periodic payment by the owner; in return, the repair facility guarantees to fix or replace the system within a specified amount of time, regardless of the problem.

Master files. In a computerized accounting system, this refers to the file containing the basic information for that module's accounts. For a general ledger, the account numbers and descriptions would be stored in the master file. For an accounts receivable module, the information about each customer would be stored in the master file.

Menu. In computer software, this term describes the process of displaying a list of choices to the operator and waiting for the operator to select one of the choices. This is much easier for the operator than having to memorize numerous different commands.

Micro. Same as microcomputer.

Micro-accounting. The keeping of a set of accounting records on a microcomputer system.

Microcomputer. The smallest type of computer. Generally developed around a single integrated circuit (called a microprocessor). This type of computer is relatively inexpensive. It is also slower and has less capacity than larger computers. The proliferation of this type of computer has resulted in an outpouring of extremely varied and innovative programs, sometimes better than the expensive programs developed for large computers.

Minicomputer. A type of computer that is larger, faster, and many times more expensive than a microcomputer. They can be used by many people simultaneously. These are relatively complex machines, harder to write programs for; they generally require a full-time staff of data-processing professionals for their care and feeding.

Modules. The accounting programs on the market are available in parts, called "modules." Each module covers one area of the accounting system; several installed on the same computer will work together (integrated). Different brands of accounting software include different functions in their various modules (i.e., all accounts receivable modules do not contain the same functions).

Multi-user microcomputer. A microcomputer that will allow several people to use it at the same time. This is appropriate when a business becomes too large for a single person to enter all of its transactions and print all of the reports.

Network. See local area network.

Operating system. A special type of program that controls the various parts of the computer, such as the disk drives, the keyboard, and the display screen. Other programs can then use the operating system, rather than having to design their own routines for those basic tasks. Users are currently expected to use the operating system for such things as formatting diskettes or making copies of diskettes.

Overdue receivables report. This reports just your overdue receivables, by customer and by aging.

Passwords. Computerized accounting systems can use passwords to prevent unauthorized access to the accounting system, or even control access to individual accounting functions. The system will ask for the password at the appropriate time; authorized users can type in the proper password; others will be prevented from carrying out any further functions. Usually you can select the passwords for each operator and each function.

Payroll. The accounting module that handles paying employees and accumulating the various categories of payroll data.

PC: Personal computer. This term indicates a computer that is used by one individual, who therefore has complete control over it. The alternative is a central computer with a data-processing staff and numerous users to be serviced.

Post. To transfer the entries for a given accounting period from journals (books of original entry) to the general ledger. Posting is also done in other areas: accounts receivable, accounts payable, payroll, inventory, and so on.

Processor. The circuit inside the computer that processes the program's instructions. Programs are lists of instructions; the processor loads, reads, and executes each instruction, one at a time.

Program diskette. A diskette which stores programs for the computer to execute. Computerized accounting systems initially consist of several program diskettes; the data diskettes that store the accounting information are created and used as needed.

Reconciliation. The bringing of two accounts or statements into agreement.

Recovery. The replacing of incorrect or questionable data with a set of correct data. The set of correct data comes from a backup operation carried out previously. Usually there is some amount of work that has been done since the last backup operation; that effort must be repeated, since it will not be included in the replacement data.

Scroll. To move data up and down on the computer screen in a continuous stream, as if the screen were a window onto a small section of a moving sheet of paper.

Single-user microcomputer. A system which is limited to the use of a single person at any one time. Several people can use the system, but they must use it one at a time.

Software. The lists of instructions that tell computer hardware what to do. Also called computer programs.

Spreadsheet. A type of software that simulates a sheet of columnar paper, with automatic calculations and easy editing. This software is widely used for financial planning and projections. Any value can easily be changed and the end results automatically recalculated.

Statement. A report listing financial accounts and their balances, usually in a conventional order and form. The standard financial statements are the Balance Sheet, the Income Statement, and the Statement of Changes in Financial Position.

Statement of changes in financial position. A standard financial statement that shows sources and uses of funds over a specified time interval.

System security. The area of protection against intentional or accidental errors, assuring that the amounts reported by the system are correct and accurate.

Terminal. A piece of computer hardware that consists mainly of a keyboard and a display screen. For a multi-user computer, multiple terminals are used to allow many users to interact with the one computer.

Tracked. The keeping of a historical record or accumulation over time. If the system tracks a customer's year-to-date purchases, it adds each additional purchase for that customer to the previous entries it has stored.

Trial balance worksheet. A listing of the total debits and the total credits of each general ledger account, for the purpose of verifying the balance between the debits and the credits, and verifying the account balances.

Update. A term used by some accounting programs to indicate the erasing of detailed transaction information, leaving just a net balance for each account. This is often done at the end of an accounting period, after all of the reports have been produced, to make room for the next period's transactions.

Vendor ledger. A listing of each vendor showing all transactions and beginning and ending balances.

White space. The area on a report that has no characters printed on it.

Word processing. Software for generating letters and reports (text).

Write operation. The process of storing information onto a floppy diskette or a hard disk.

INDEX